WITH THE WORD OF GOD

WITH THE Word of God
– LECTIO DIVINA –

A guide for prayer in school, home and parish

Jude Groden, RSM and Christopher O'Donnell, O.CARM

McCrimmons

*In memory of our parents
and of those who brought us to faith.*

First published in United Kingdom in 2003 by
McCrimmon Publishing Co. Ltd.,
10-12 High Street, Great Wakering, Essex SS3 0EQ
Email: mccrimmons@dial.pipex.com
Website: www.mccrimmons.com

© 2003 Sr. Jude Groden and Rev. Christopher O'Donnell

ISBN 0 85597 646 2

Acknowledgements

Scriptural extracts are taken from the *Good News Bible* published by The Bible Societies / Harper Collins Publishers Ltd., UK. © American Bible Society 1966, 1971, 1976, 1992

Extracts taken from *A Treasury of Prayer*, T. Castle, ed., © 1983 Hodder and Stoughton Ltd, 338 Euston Road, London NW1 3BH.

Extracts taken from *The Catholic Prayer from Downside Abbey*, D. Foster, ed., © 1999 T. & T. Clark, 59 George Street, Edinburgh, EH2 2LQ

Extracts taken from *The Saints Prayerbook*, A. F. Chiffolo, ed., © 1998 Canterbury Press, St Mary's Works, St. Mary's Plain, Norwich, Norfolk NR3 3BH.

Extracts taken from *An Alphabet of Prayer 2001*, © Redemption Publications, Alphonsus House, Chawton, Hampshire, GU34 3HQ.

Every effort has been made to trace the owners of copyright material and we hope that no copyright has been infringed. Pardon is sought and apology made if the contrary be the case, and a correction will be made in any reprint of this book.

Illustrations on pages 41, 58, 63, 64, 65 are by Peter Edwards.
All other illustrations are by the the Benedictine Sisters of Turvey Abbey.

Cover design and photograph by Alan Hencher
Page design and layout by Nick Snode
Typeset in 11 and 11.5pt Verdana
Printed and bound by Thanet Press Ltd., Margate, Kent.

Contents

Foreword

There are many books on prayer. Indeed the contemporary interest in prayer and spirituality is one of the most significant and hopeful signs in the Church today. How I pray reflects how I believe. That is why prayer is so inspired by Scripture. As St Ambrose said: "We speak to Him when we pray; we listen to Him when we read divine Scripture."

Sr Jude Groden is a Mercy Sister and a member of the Brentwood Religious Education Service (BRES). She has written this book along with an Irish Carmelite theologian from the Milltown Institute, Dublin, Father Christopher O'Donnell, who has frequently lectured in this diocese. The book they have produced involved their combined gifts of an educationalist and a theologian.

I am particularly pleased to welcome a book on prayer and Scripture.
A recent instruction from the Holy See on *Popular Piety and Liturgy* has spoken extensively about praying with Scripture. It notes, "Since the Church is built on, and grows through, listening to the Word of God, the Christian faithful should acquire a familiarity with Sacred Scripture and be imbued with its spirit."
The document goes on to say, "The Bible offers an inexhaustible source of inspiration to popular piety, as well as unrivalled forms of prayer and thematic subjects." (#87). My favourite definition of prayer is: "Making ourselves present to the presence of God." What better way of doing this than through God's Word in Scripture.

† Thomas McMahon.

Bishop of Brentwood

Introduction

PRAYING WITH SCRIPTURE

It is common to hear about a hunger for spirituality, or even a hunger for prayer. How are we to satisfy our hunger?
If we have not eaten for a long while, then a hamburger at a fast food outlet will be very satisfying. But we are being warned by government and health authorities that too much fast food is not good: it is not a balanced diet, it puts on the wrong kind of weight. It is all right to try one kind of cooking, e.g. ethnic, or occasional take-aways, but we need a healthy pattern of eating for everyday health and growth.

So too in our spiritual life. We can occasionally try various kinds of prayer. But we need some established pattern that we can fall back on, that will sustain us in bad weather and fair weather. Some people go around the prayer garden like a bee. They go to a flower and suck it dry; then they move off to another flower, hoping for more honey. They hop from one way of prayer to another, without staying long enough to find the true riches in any form of prayer.

One question that we can ask ourselves is, why might we need a new method? This volume of scriptural reflections draws on an ancient tradition of prayer, which has become very popular in recent decades. It sets down the Scripture as an anchor for prayer. We will of course pray in other ways, such as attending our church for Sunday worship, or other favourite devotions, or prayer moments like a blessing before meals.

Bible and Life

Thirty years ago the Second Vatican Council warned us: "One of the gravest errors of our time is the split between the faith which many profess, and the practice of their daily lives" (*Church in the Modern World* GS 43). The task is to integrate religion and life. The glue that keeps them together is prayer.
Life draws us to prayer so that we can get a better perspective on situations; faith offers a new vision of reality.
The main place where this fusion occurs is prayer. It would seem that prayer based on the Scriptures would have an immediate advantage in drawing us from the world to the vision of faith, and of pointing our faith vision to the realities of daily life. The recent Vatican Instruction, *Popular Piety and the Liturgy* (2001) states, "It is impossible to imagine a Christian prayer without direct or indirect reference to the Sacred Scripture" (#12). It also deplored the dualism between liturgy and piety that developed in the Middle Ages. One of the reasons for this development is said to be "lack of sufficient knowledge of the Scriptures on the part not only of the laity, but of many clerics and religious" (#30). It strongly recommends the integration of the Word of God and popular piety.

How to read the Bible

People may well hear such exhortations to use the Scriptures more, but react like the Ethiopian who said to Philip, "How can I understand unless someone shows me?" (Acts 8:31). The Bible is a complex book; or, rather, more than seventy books, all of various kinds. It takes years of study to become a true scriptural scholar or exegete. Their work is essential for the Church, and it gradually proliferates through the Christian community. Few nowadays would think that Moses put pen to paper and wrote fully himself the first five books of the Bible.

Catholics are told that access to the Scripture ought to be open to all the faithful (Vatican II, *Constitution on Revelation* DV 22). Is there not a danger of going astray when ordinary, non-experts, read the Scripture? There is indeed. But we are also told that the magisterium alone gives authoritative interpretations of the sacred text (DV 10). Some theologians suggest that there are only two or three such authoritative interpretations.
Is it dangerous then to read the Bible? Yes, but we can be protected by our personal faith and by using ways of reading the Bible which, with the help of the Holy Spirit, will lead us to its meaning.

We need to realise that we are not alone in reading the Scriptures. We have the author of the Bible, the Holy Spirit, to help us. If we are to allow our Helper and Guide to lead us into the depths of the Word of God, then we need to avoid bringing too much clutter or baggage to the text. We are best with the text in openness to the Spirit.

An ancient and new method

For over one thousand years a method has developed that allows such simple reading that allows for the guidance of the Scripture. It is a method, not an elaborate set of rules or a set of hoops that we have to navigate. But a method is helpful. We have all had the experience of opening the Bible and sitting there with no thoughts coming. It is then easy to read the introduction to the translation we are using, look at the maps, admire the cover – all nice things to do, but hardly praying!

The ancient method was called *Lectio Divina* or Divine Reading. It was a way of praying with the Scriptures that proceeds in a few very natural steps. We should always begin with some prayer. St Teresa of Avila suggested beginning with the "I confess," thus recognising our sins and preparing to come to God. We could make up such a prayer based on the penitential rite at the liturgy; we look at ourselves and God and say, "Lord have mercy." One could then ask for the help of the Holy Spirit.

The method begins with reading a text. It is useful to read out loud. Here is God's Word. He is speaking to me or to the group that is praying. In the Eastern Churches people call the Bible "God's love-letter to his people." The most natural thing then is to ask, what is the text saying? We read it carefully, looking for the story or the meaning of the passage. It is helpful to watch out for details, to keep an eye on the verbs, which tell us who is acting, or what is happening. Silence is important, as it can take time for us to see the details.

If we have the Word of God addressed to us, there is a natural progression to another stage. We should surely wonder, what is it saying to me, to us now? If we have not had the first stage of careful reading of the text, we will not have good reflection. It takes time to allow the text to speak personally. We can think of ourselves in the scene, we can hear the words as addressed to us, we can apply it to our life situation. The point here is making the Word of God personal.

But there is surely another step we can take. We are in dialogue with God. In the first stage we are trying to understand the text with the help of the Holy Spirit.

Then we hope that the Spirit will give us ideas of how that text related to us. These two steps focus more on God speaking to us: we are not, however, wholly passive, we are listening and alert, but also thinking. Now it is natural that we respond to God. We can speak to God in our own words. We can use a few words, phrases from Scripture or from well-loved prayers.

The important thing is that we make these our own.

Finally, we can stay with the text. We have been listening, thinking, speaking. Now is the time for rest. We look back over the text and take some idea that has struck or is just now striking us. An image might be of having a last look at a nice view before moving on, or picking a single flower from a garden or a field.

Alone or in groups

This simple method or prayer in four stages – reading, reflecting, responding, and resting – can be used when we are praying alone or in groups. If we are alone, we can divide up our time

according to the way in which we feel drawn. If we wonder how long we should stay with any section, the answer might be "a little longer". Sometimes it is when we think there is nothing more to see or find, that we get another insight or thought.

If we are praying in groups then one person can lead the session and quietly suggest moving on to each phase. It is important that the person who is leading is not seen as an expert. We are at prayer, not at class. We do not ask questions and expect some person cleverer than ourselves to have the answer. We are there to listen to God who will be speaking to us through others. Questions can be asked later. We should try to create a welcoming atmosphere in which each person will feel that his or her contribution will be received with respect.

Using this book

This book is offered as an introduction or guide to praying with Scripture. It is designed for use alone or with others such as parish societies, or Bible groups. It is also very suitable for schools. The texts are chosen to reflect the great concerns of the Old and New Testaments and to present some of the principal figures of each. The compilers of the text have kept an eye continually on the *Here I Am* religious education programme. Each text has an introduction, which sets the context of the passage. It also relates it to the appropriate *Here I Am* topics.

After the text one will find the four stages of the scriptural method of *lectio divina*: Reading, Reflection, Response, Rest. In each section there are leading questions that will help the person or the group to focus: what is the text saying? what does it mean to me/to us? making up or recalling some prayer response; remaining with the text.

With each section there are possible prompts. These are only indicators and should be ignored if a person or the group has other ideas to support the stage of prayer. On the other hand they may help give a line of thought that people would like to explore further.

Finally, there is a suggested concluding prayer. But there are innumerable possibilities of other prayers, phrases from Scripture, set prayers, lines from hymns, or something composed spontaneously.

The compilers of this book hope that it may help people to set out on the voyage of biblical prayer. The method has been found extremely helpful in the preparation of homilies. It can help with the prayerful reading of Scripture that is recommended by the recent Vatican document, on popular piety, which is quoting the Second Vatican Council: "Prayer should accompany the reading of Sacred Scripture so that a dialogue takes place" (#88; DV 25).

Jeremiah's call

INTRODUCTION

■ *Scripture*. The Prophet Jeremiah was called by God about 627 BC.
He was a reluctant prophet. God's call helped Jeremiah to know himself.

■ *Here I Am*. The greatest learning that will take place for us will be the journey of knowing ourselves. It has been said that when speaking about the spiritual life, there are three important truths I must know about myself.
  1) I am a sinner and selfish.
  2) I am weak.
  3) I am holy.
Discovering ourselves is a life-long task.

SCRIPTURE   Jeremiah 1: 4-10

THE LORD said to me, "I chose you before I gave you life. And before you were born I selected you to be a prophet to the nations."
I answered, "Sovereign Lord, I don't know how to speak; I am too young." But the Lord said to me, "Do not say that you are too young, but go to the people I send you to, and tell them everything I command you to say. Do not be afraid of them, for I will be with you to protect you. I, the Lord, have spoken!" Then the Lord stretched out his hand touched my lips, and said to me, "Listen, I am giving you the words you must speak. Today I give you authority over nations and kingdoms to uproot and to pull down, to destroy and to overthrow, to build and to plant."

1. READING

What is going on?

Read the text and ask, what is going on? What strikes you about this passage? Details? Actions?

Possible prompts:

- I chose you before I gave you life.
- Before you were born I selected you to be a prophet to the nations.
- Go to the people I send you to and tell them everything I command you to say.
- Do not be afraid of them, I will be with you to protect you.
- Listen, I am giving you the words you must speak.
- They will not defeat you.

2. REFLECTION

What does it mean for us?

Read the text again. What phrase do you like in the text and why? What word attracts you? How does the text speak to you in the various places and situations in which you find yourself?

Possible prompts:

- The Lord chose us before we were born.
- Do we hear, "Do not be afraid..."?
- Do we feel his protecting love?
- Speaking his words to others.
- The Word of God coming to me.

3. RESPONSE

Making some prayers

Read the text again. We have heard God's Word and we have tried to see what it means. We can talk to Jesus about his message. It can be a prayer you know, or one you make up.

Possible prompts:

- Thank you for choosing me to speak your words to others.
- Give me the courage of Jeremiah the prophet.
- When life is difficult, help me hear you say, "Do not be afraid."

4. REST

Enjoy the text

Read the text again.

Pause – a minute or two of silence with the text.

Invite pupils to take away a few words from this time of reflection, prayer or meditation as a message for today.

- The Lord chose me even before I was born.
- God's protecting love is with me always.

A CONCLUDING PRAYER

Father, we are your chosen people.
May we live with compassion, kindness, humility and patience.
May we forgive each other as you forgive us.
May we live with the love which brings everyone together in perfect harmony.
May the peace of Christ reign in our hearts.
May the words we speak and the deeds we perform in your Son's name tell you of our thanks and praise.

Annunciation to Mary

INTRODUCTION

■ *Scripture.* At the very end of the Old Testament God's plan for the world was ready. It involves Mary being asked to be the Mother of the Messiah, who was the Son of God.

■ *Here I Am.* It is often said that all endings are new beginnings. Each moment of each day we stand at the gateway of new beginnings. Beginnings are times of hope, high expectations and great enthusiasm. Beginnings can also be occasions of fear. As we meditate on the following, we meet with Mary the Lord of all beginnings

SCRIPTURE   Luke 1: 26-38

I N THE sixth month of Elizabeth's pregnancy, God sent the angel Gabriel to a town in Galilee named Nazareth. He had a message for a girl promised in marriage to a man named Joseph, who was a descendant of King David. The girl's name was Mary. The angel came to her and said, "Peace be with you! The Lord is with you and has greatly blessed you!" Mary was deeply troubled by the angel's message and she wondered what his words meant. "Mary; God had been gracious to you, You will become pregnant and give birth to a son, and you will name him Jesus. He will be great and will be called the Son of the Most High God. The Lord God will make him a king, as his ancestor David was, and he will be the king of all descendants of Jacob for ever; his kingdom will never end!" Mary said to the angel, "I am a virgin. How, then, can this be?" The angel answered, "The Holy Spirit will come on you, and God's power will rest upon you. For this reason the holy child will be called the Son of God. Remember your relative, Elizabeth. It is said that she cannot have children, but she herself is now six months pregnant, even though she is very old. For there is nothing that God cannot do." "I am the Lord's servant, " said Mary; "may it happen to me as you have said." And the angel left her.

1. READING

What is going on?

Read the text and ask, what is going on? What strikes you about this passage? Details? Actions?

Possible prompts:

- God sends an angel with a message to Mary, an engaged young woman.
- The angel's greeting.
- Why was Mary puzzled and upset?
- The angel's reaction and explanation.
- The Holy Spirit will come upon you and God's power will rest upon you.

2. REFLECTION

What does it mean for us?

Read the text again. What phrase do you like in the text and why? What word attracts you? How does the text speak to you in the various places and situations you find yourself?

Possible prompts:

- God comes also to us?
- God says: "Do not be afraid."
- Have we ever felt the power of God's love resting on us?
- To be like Mary.
- God can do everything.
- Do we say with Mary – We are the servants of the Lord?

3. RESPONSE

Making some prayers

Read the text again. We have heard God's Word and we have tried to see what it means. We can talk to Jesus about his message. It can be a prayer you know, or one you make up.

Possible prompts:

- Thanks for messages of love.
- Thanks for blessings.
- Thanks for beginnings.
- Thanks for relief of fear.

4. REST

Enjoy the text

Read the text again.

Pause – a minute or two of silence with the text. Invite pupils to take away a few words from this time of reflection, prayer or meditation as a message for today.

- "Peace be with you."
- "Do not be afraid."
- "The Lord is with you and has greatly blessed you."

A CONCLUDING PRAYER from the Angelus

The angel of the Lord declared unto Mary, and she conceived by the Holy Spirit. Hail Mary...

Behold the handmaid of the Lord. Be it done unto me according to your word. Hail Mary...

The Word was made flesh and dwelt among us, Hail Mary...

Pray for us, O Holy Mother of God: That we may be made worthy of the promises of Christ.

Blessing of children

INTRODUCTION

■ *Scripture.* In the Gospel we see Jesus' love for children. We also find that the ease, trust and simplicity of children are for Jesus the ideal way to come to him.

■ *Here I Am*: The birth and arrival of a baby is one of the greatest signs and wonder of God's love, not only to the family but also to all around. It unites a family in great rejoicing and happiness. In this meditation we meet Jesus who blesses the babies and asks us to trust him as children do.

SCRIPTURE

Luke 18: 15-1

SOME PEOPLE brought their babies to Jesus for him to place his hands on them. The disciples saw them and scolded them for doing so, but Jesus called the children to him and said, "Let the children come to me and do not stop them, because the Kingdom of God belongs to such as these. Remember this! Whoever does not receive the Kingdom of God like a child will never enter it."

1. READING

What is going on?

Read the text and ask, what is going on? What strikes you about this passage? Details? Actions?

Possible prompts:

- Bringing babies to Jesus; why?
- The disciples upset.
- What does Jesus do and say?
- The word about the Kingdom.

16

2. REFLECTION

What does it mean for us?

Read the text again. What phrase do you like in the text and why? What word attracts you? How does the text speak to you in the various places and situations you find yourself?

Possible prompts:

- Who has brought us to Jesus?
- Do we hear God's call to us to come to him?
- What is important about the way we love Jesus and his message?
- We must not stop others or keep them away from Jesus.

3. RESPONSE

Making some prayers

Read the text again. We have heard God's Word and we have tried to see what it means. We can talk to Jesus about his message. It can be a prayer you know or one you make up.

Possible prompts:

- Thank you for all your blessings on all of us.
- Help our families to love you more.
- Show us how to trust you.
- Protect all babies and all who love them.

4. REST

Enjoy the text

Read the text again.

Pause – a minute or two of silence with the text.

Invite pupils to take away a few words from this time of reflection, prayer or meditation as a message for today.

- The greatest is the one who becomes like a child.
- Whoever welcomes a child welcomes me.

A CONCLUDING PRAYER

I love you, Jesus,
My love above all things.
I repent with my whole heart of having offended you.
Never permit me to separate myself from you again;
Grant that I may love you always,
And then do with me what you will.

St Alphonsus

Christian living

INTRODUCTION

■ *Scripture*. This short text from the Letter to the Colossians gives us a picture of how the Christian family and community are to live.

■ *Here I Am*. In our homes and families we learn, experience and test out ways of loving. For some, these early days of childhood are rich and beautiful; for others life is harsh and painful. In this meditation we are offered a map to help us live happy, loving lives and how to treat others.

SCRIPTURE

Colossians 3: 12-1

YOU ARE the people of God; he loved you and chose you for his own. So then, you must clothe yourselves with compassion, kindness, humility, gentleness and patience. Be tolerant with one another and forgive one another whenever any of you has a complaint against someone else. You must forgive one another just as the Lord has forgiven you. And to all these qualities add love, which binds all things together in perfect unity. The peace that Christ gives is to guide you in the decisions you make for it is to this peace that God has called you together in the one body. And be thankful. Christ's message in all its richness must live in your hearts. Teach and instruct each other with all wisdom. Sing psalms, hymns, and sacred songs; sing to God with thanksgiving in your hearts. Everything you do or say, then, should be done in the name of the Lord Jesus, as you give thanks through him to God the Father.

1. READING

What is going on?

Read the text and ask, what is going on? What strikes you about this passage? Details? Actions?

Possible prompts:

- God loved and chose you for his own.
- Wearing compassion, kindness, humility, gentleness and patience like clothes.
- Tolerance, forgiveness and love bring us together.
- The peace of Christ guides us.
- Thankfulness makes our hearts lighter.

2. REFLECTION

What does it mean for us?

Read the text again. What phrase do you like in the text and why? What word attracts you? How does the text speak to you in the various places and situations you find yourself?

Possible prompts:

- How do we score in compassion, kindness, humility, and gentleness?
- Tolerance and forgiveness are not easy.
- Can these make us feel good?
- Are we thankful?

3. RESPONSE

Making some prayers

Read the text again. We have heard God's Word and we have tried to see what it means. We can talk to Jesus about his message. It can be a prayer you know or one you make up.

Possible prompts:

- Thank you for loving us as we are and calling us into your family.
- Help us to be compassionate, kind, gentle and patient with others.
- Strengthen us to forgive as the Lord forgives us.
- Support our efforts to be peace-loving and peacemakers.
- Make us more thankful.

4. REST

Enjoy the text

Read the text again.

Pause – a minute or two of silence with the text.

Invite pupils to take away a few words from this time of reflection, prayer or meditation as a message for today.

- Loved by God.
- Peace and gentleness.
- God teaching us how to live.

A CONCLUDING PRAYER

God be in my head
And my understanding.
God be in my eyes
And in my looking.
God be in my mouth
And in my speaking.
God be in my heart
And in my thinking.
God be at mine end
And at my departing.

Sarum Primer

Invited by God

INTRODUCTION

■ *Scripture*. The people in Jesus' time loved weddings – nice food, meet relatives, have a good time for days. So a wedding is used as a symbol of the good time we have and will have as we enjoy God's blessings.

■ *Here I Am*. Invitations of various kinds are thoughtful gestures, which are usually prompted by good intentions. Some we happily accept, others we decline. In the following meditation on the wedding feast we meet Jesus who is always offering us an invitation enjoy his many gifts.

SCRIPTURE

Matthew 22: 1-14

JESUS again used parables in talking to the people. "The Kingdom of heaven is like this. Once there was a king who prepared a wedding feast for his son. He sent his servants to tell the invited guests to come to the feast, but they did not want to come. So he sent other servants with this message for the guests: 'My feast is ready now, my bullocks and prize calves have been butchered, and everything is ready. Come to the wedding feast!' But the invited guests paid no attention and went about their business: one went to his farm, another to his shop, while others grabbed the servants, beat them, and killed them. The king was very angry, so he sent his soldiers, who killed those murderers and burnt down their city. Then he called his servants and said to them 'My wedding feast is ready, but the people I invited did not deserve it. Now go to the main streets and invite to the feast as many people as you find.' So the servants went out into the streets and gathered all the people they could find, good and bad alike; and the wedding hall was filled with people..." And Jesus concluded, "Many are invited, but few are chosen."

1. READING

What is going on?

Read the text and ask, what is going on? What strikes you about this passage? Details? Actions?

Possible prompts:

- The feast was ready but the invited guests did not want to come.
- Had they good excuses for insulting the king?
- He decides to invite others, who will be glad of the invitation.
- "Many are invited, but few are chosen."

2. REFLECTION

What does it mean for us?

Read the text again. What phrase do you like in the text and why? What word attracts you? How does the text speak to you in the various places and situations you find yourself?

Possible prompts:

- Jesus invites us to the feast of his love – do we accept?
- Do we listen to God's invitations to be loving and kind at home and at school?
- Do we make excuses for being cold and sulky when God invites us to do something?
- God wants us to enjoy ourselves and shows us how.

3. RESPONSE

Making some prayers

Read the text again. We have heard God's Word and we have tried to see what it means. We can talk to Jesus about his message. It can be a prayer you know or one you make up.

Possible prompts:

- Lord, thank you for your constant invitation to follow you in love.
- Forgive the times we ignore your invitation.
- Strengthen all who feel rejected.
- Open our hearts to receive your gifts.

4. REST

Enjoy the text

Read the text again.

Pause – a minute or two of silence with the text.

Invite pupils to take away a few words from this time of reflection, prayer or meditation as a message for today.

- God's invitations.
- Our excuses.
- We can enjoy ourselves and be good.

A CONCLUDING PRAYER

We thank you, Father, for inviting us into your family in baptism
  and to enjoy meeting your Son Jesus
  at Mass when you teach and feed us.
May we be positive about life
  and enjoy your many gifts.
Through Christ our Lord. Amen.

David and Jonathan

■ *Scripture*: The greatest story of friendship in the Old Testament is that between Jonathan, the king's son, and David, who was out of favour with the king. Jonathan protected David even at the risk of his own life.

■ *Here I Am*: Friendship is a great gift. In schools and life in general we speak or think of friendship at four levels: friendship with God, friendship with others, friendship with self, friendship with the world. We are truly blessed if we have faithful and true friends who are loyal and support us in good and difficult times. Friendship also makes demands. Here we consider the lovely friendship between Jonathan and David.

SCRIPTURE

1 Samuel 20: 2-14, 23

JONATHAN said to David, "God forbid that you should die! My father tells me everything he does, important or not, and he would not hide this from me. It isn't true!" But David answered, "Your father knows very well how much you like me, and he has decided not to let you know what he plans to do, because you would be deeply hurt. I swear to you by the living Lord that I am only a step away from death!" Jonathan said, "I'll do anything you want." Tomorrow is the New Moon Festival," David replied, "and I am supposed to eat with the king. But if it's all right with you, I will go and hide in the fields until the evening of the day after tomorrow. If your father notices that I am not at table, tell him that I begged your permission to hurry home to Bethlehem, since it's the time for the annual sacrifice there for my whole family. If he says, 'All right,' I will be safe; but if he becomes angry, you will know that he is determined to harm me. Please do me this favour, and keep the sacred promise you made to me. But if I am guilty, kill me yourself! Why take me to your father to be killed?" "Don't even think such a thing!" Jonathan answered. "If I knew for certain that my father was determined to harm you, wouldn't I tell you?" David then asked, "Who will let me know if you father answers you angrily?" "Let's go out to the fields," Jonathan answered. So they went, and Jonathan said to David, "May the Lord God of Israel be our witness! At this time tomorrow and on the following day I will question my father. If his attitude towards you is good, I will send you word. If he intends to harm you, may the Lord be with you as he was with my father! And if I remain alive, please keep your sacred promise and be loyal to me... As for the promise we made to each other, the Lord will make sure that we keep it for ever."

1. READING

What is going on?

Read the text and ask, what is going on? What strikes you about this passage? Details? Actions?

Possible prompts:

- The close friendship between David and Jonathan.
- David is aware that King Saul, Jonathan's father, is bitter and envious and wants to kill him.
- Jonathan is loyal and faithful; he protects David.
- Jonathan places himself at personal risk for his friend.

2. REFLECTION

What does it mean for us?

Read the text again. What phrase do you like in the text and why? What word attracts you? How does the text speak to you in the various places and situations you find yourself?

Possible prompts:

- Are we faithful and loyal friends?
- Do we want the best for our friends or are we envious at times?
- What happens when friendship becomes difficult or painful?
- Do we protect our friends or let them down?
- Are we grateful for the bonds of friendship?

3. RESPONSE

Making some prayers

Read the text again. We have heard God's Word and we have tried to see what it means. We can talk to Jesus about his message. It can be a prayer you know or one you make up.

Possible prompts:

- Thank you for the blessing of having friends and friendship.
- Help us to be true and faithful friends.
- May we always forgive those who hurt us and let us down.
- Heal people who are bitter and envious.
- Be close to all who are finding love and friendship difficult.

4. REST

Enjoy the text

Read the text again.

Pause – a minute or two of silence with the text.

Invite pupils to take away a few words from this time of reflection, prayer or meditation as a message for today.

- Good friends.
- Friendship as receiving and giving.
- Working at building friendship.

A CONCLUDING PRAYER

Jesus said, "I call you friends."
May I be his loyal friend. Amen.

Becoming Christians

INTRODUCTION

■ *Scripture*. St Paul found some people at Ephesus who believed in Jesus, but had not received the sacraments of baptism and confirmation. He knew this because they never seemed to have heard of the Holy Spirit who makes us Christians.

■ *Here I Am*: Initiation is about beginnings. Christian beginnings are through the sacraments of baptism, confirmation and Eucharist. To be a full Christian we need all three. But there is also a sense that initiation is ongoing: we must always be going deeper into the grace of baptism; we continually need more and more of the confirmation gift of the Holy Spirit; we need the Bread of Heaven, the Body of the Lord, to keep us going on the pilgrimage of life.

SCRIPTURE   Acts 19: 1-6

PAUL TRAVELLED through the interior of the province and arrived at Ephesus. There he found some disciples and asked them, "Did you receive the Holy Spirit when you became believers?" "We have not even heard that there is a Holy Spirit," they answered. "Well, then, what kind of baptism did you receive?" Paul asked. "The baptism of John," they replied. Paul said, "The baptism of John was for those who turned from their sins; and he told the people of Israel to believe in the one who was coming after him – that is, in Jesus." When they heard that they were baptized in the name of the Lord Jesus. Paul placed his hands on them, and the Holy Spirit came upon them.

1. READING

What is going on?

Read the text and ask, what is going on? What strikes you about this passage? Details? Actions?

Possible prompts:

- Why was Paul surprised?
- Who was John and what was his baptism?
- What is the Holy Spirit?
- What did Jesus mean for the people, and for Paul?

2. REFLECTION

What does it mean for us?

Read the text again. What phrase do you like in the text and why? What word attracts you? How does the text speak to you in the various places and situations you find yourself?

Possible prompts:

- Where were you baptised?
- What does being a Christian mean to you?
- Can you remember your confirmation or are you looking forward to your confirmation?
- What difference do you think confirmation makes?

3. RESPONSE

Making some prayers

Read the text again. We have heard God's Word and we have tried to see what it means. We can talk to Jesus about his message. It can be a prayer you know or one you make up.

Possible prompts:

- Thank you God for the gift of baptism.
- Help me to understand your gifts and to use them.
- The Holy Spirit teaches me about Jesus.
- Come to us, Jesus.
- Come, Holy Spirit.

4. REST

Enjoy the text

Read the text again.

Pause – a minute or two of silence with the text.

Invite pupils to take away a few words from this time of reflection, prayer or meditation as a message for today.

- Jesus and the Holy Spirit.
- It's great to be a Christian!

A CONCLUDING PRAYER

Come, Holy Spirit,
fill the hearts of your people
and light up in them the fire
of your love.

Send forth your Spirit, Lord,
and they shall be created.
And you shall make new the face
of the earth.

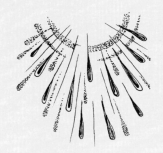

Baptism

INTRODUCTION

■ *Scripture*: When he was about thirty, Jesus went to John who was baptising people to make them ready for the Messiah. Jesus himself is baptised and this begins his public life and ministry, which will lead to his death for us.

■ *Here I Am*: We are familiar with signs and notices that tell us something. There are also signs like shaking hands.

Sending a Christmas or birthday card that tells people that we value them. There are also spiritual signs: these are ordinary things that Jesus uses to make us holy, like water in baptism, oil at confirmation and bread and wine to become changed into his Body and Blood. Here we consider the signs of baptism.

SCRIPTURE

Luke 3: 21-22

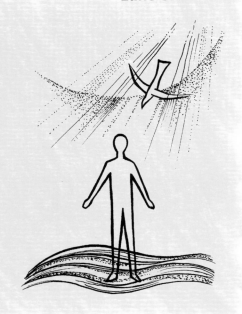

AFTER all the people had been baptised, Jesus also was baptised. While he was praying, heaven was opened, and the Holy Spirit came down upon him in bodily form like a dove, and a voice came from heaven, "You are my own dear Son. I am pleased with you."

1. READING

What is going on?

Read the text and ask, what is going on? What strikes you about this passage? Details? Actions?

Possible prompts:

- All the people being baptised.
- Jesus there and asking for baptism.
- The signs from heaven.
- The voice and the dove.

2. REFLECTION

What does it mean for us?

Read the text again. What phrase do you like in the text and why? What word attracts you? How does the text speak to you in the various places and situations you find yourself?

Possible prompts:

- Was our baptism like that?
- The Trinity at our baptism: Father, Son, Spirit.
- Do we hear God speak those words, "You are my dear son or daughter."?
- We are God's dear children.
- God says also to us: "I am pleased with you."

3. RESPONSE

Making some prayers

Read the text again. We have heard God's Word and we have tried to see what it means. We can talk to Jesus about his message. It can be a prayer you know or one you make up.

Possible prompts:

- Thank you God for my baptism.
- May I know the beauty of my baptism.
- Reward with your blessing our parents, godparents and those who prepare people for baptism.
- God our Father, Jesus our Brother, Holy Spirit our Friend, bless us.
- Thank you Lord, for all who are signs and symbols of your love.

4. REST

Enjoy the text

Read the text again.

Pause – a minute or two of silence with the text.

Invite pupils to take away a few words from this time of reflection, prayer or meditation as a message for today.

- I am God's son or daughter.
- God loves to look at me.

A CONCLUDING PRAYER

Glory be to the Father,
and to the Son and to the Holy Spirit,
as it was in the beginning,
is now, and ever shall be,
world without end. Amen.

Christmas

INTRODUCTION

■ *Scripture*: At the small town of Bethlehem God's plan came into being. The Son of God was to become man to save all of us. The first Christmas tells us so much about God's plans, what is important to him, the greatness of his love.

■ *Here I Am*: Birthdays are important moments and occasions. They are celebrations of our lives. Certain birthdays are marked out from others, but all are occasions to celebrate the gifts of love and life. Here we think about the birth of Jesus at the first Christmas.

SCRIPTURE   Luke 2: 6-11, 13-14

WHEN JOSEPH AND MARY were in Bethlehem, the time came for her to have her baby. She gave birth to her first son, wrapped him in strips of cloth and laid him in a manger – there was no room for them to stay in the inn. There were some shepherds in that part of the country who were spending the night in the fields, taking care of their flocks. An angel of the Lord appeared to them, and the glory of the Lord shone over them. They were terribly afraid, but the angel said to them, "Don't be afraid! I am here with good news for you, which will bring great joy to all the people. This very day in David's town, your Saviour was born, Christ the Lord..." Suddenly a great army of heaven's angels appeared with the angel, singing praises to God: "Glory to God in the highest heaven, and peace on earth to those with whom he is pleased!"

1. READING

What is going on?

Read the text and ask, what is going on? What strikes you about this passage? Details? Actions?

Possible prompts:

- Mary expecting her child.
- No room for them to stay.
- The birth of God's Son in a stable.
- Shepherds and angels.

2. REFLECTION

What does it mean for us?

Read the text again. What phrase do you like in the text and why? What word attracts you? How does the text speak to you in the various places and situations you find yourself?

Possible prompts:

- Imagine being there: what would you think of saying?
- When we see the word "Christmas" we may not think about Bethlehem!
- There are many people with no place to stay.
- What would be a good way of saying "Happy Birthday" to Jesus?

3. RESPONSE

Making some prayers

Read the text again. We have heard God's Word and we have tried to see what it means. We can talk to Jesus about his message. It can be a prayer you know or one you make up.

Possible prompts:

- Thank you, Jesus, Mary and Joseph.
- Bless new mothers and their babies.
- Comfort the homeless and refugees.
- Thank you, God, for my own birthdays.

4. REST

Enjoy the text

Read the text again.

Pause – a minute or two of silence with the text.

Invite pupils to take away a few words from this time of reflection, prayer or meditation as a message for today.

- Linger in the stable.
- Relax with Jesus, Mary and Joseph.

A CONCLUDING PRAYER

O come let us adore him,
O come let us adore him,
O come let us adore him,
Christ the Lord.

John the Baptist

INTRODUCTION

■ *Scripture*: John, the cousin of Jesus had two names. He was called "the Precursor" because he went ahead of Jesus to prepare for the Lord. He was also called "the Baptist" because he invited people to confess their sins, change their lives, and be baptised in the river Jordan as a sign of their new life.

■ *Here I Am*: Each moment of our lives is a preparation for something. We prepare

for work, for school, for swimming; an artist has to prepare the canvas for painting. We prepare for special events, eg birthdays, First Communion, confirmation or a wedding. Preparations are made for examinations, for new schools or moving to a new home. There are, then, many different kinds of preparations. In this meditation we think of the way God made preparations for the Good News through John the Baptist.

SCRIPTURE

Mark 1: 1-8

THIS IS the Good News about Jesus Christ, the Son of God. It began as the prophet Isaiah had written: "God said, 'I will send my messenger ahead of you to clear the way for you.' Someone is shouting in the desert, 'Get the road ready for the Lord; Make a straight path for him to travel!'" So John appeared in the desert, baptising and preaching. "Turn away from your sins and be baptised," he told the people "and God will forgive your sins." Many people from the province of Judaea and the city of Jerusalem went out to hear John. They confessed their sins, and he baptised them in the River Jordan. John wore clothes made of camel's hair with a leather belt round his waist, and his food was locusts and wild honey. He announced to the people, "The man who will come after me is much greater than I am, I am not good enough even to bend down and untie his sandals. I baptise you with water, but he will baptise you with the Holy Spirit."

1. READING

What is going on?

Read the text and ask, what is going on? What strikes you about this passage? Details? Actions?

Possible prompts:

- God sending his messenger.
- A road for God to travel to his people.
- Turn away from your sins and be baptised.
- God will forgive you.
- Jesus is greater than John; he will baptise with the Holy Spirit.

2. REFLECTION

What does it mean for us?

Read the text again. What phrase do you like in the text and why? What word attracts you? How does the text speak to you in the various places and situations you find yourself?

Possible prompts:

- Are we always aware of God going before us and clearing a way for us?
- Do we clear a way for God to come to us?
- Do we prepare to meet Jesus in different ways?
- Do we ever listen to Jesus saying, "Turn away from your sins."
- It's great to hear: "God will forgive you."

3. RESPONSE

Making some prayers

Read the text again. We have heard God's Word and we have tried to see what it means. We can talk to Jesus about his message. It can be a prayer you know or one you make up.

Possible prompts:

- Prepare my heart for you, O Lord.
- Show me the road to you.
- Let me always remember the words, "Turn away from sin."
- May I always turn to you and seek your forgiveness.
- Thank you for all your gifts.

4. REST

Enjoy the text

Read the text again.

Pause – a minute or two of silence with the text.

Invite pupils to take away a few words from this time of reflection, prayer or meditation as a message for today.

- God comes to me.
- I should prepare for his coming.

A CONCLUDING PRAYER

Be a bright flame before me.
Be a guiding star above me.
Be a smooth path below me,
Be a kindly shepherd behind me.
Today – tomorrow – and forever.

St Columba

Epiphany

INTRODUCTION

■ *Scripture:* At Bethlehem Jesus was shown first to the Jews represented by the shepherds. Then wise men from the east came who stand for all foreign peoples.

■ *Here I Am:* We receive and offer gifts on different occasions: birthdays, baptism, Christmas, anniversaries etc. Some gifts we treasure more than others, not because of what they cost, but because we value the person who gave it. In this meditation we journey with the visitors from the east bringing their gifts to Jesus.

SCRIPTURE

Matthew 2: 1-3, 5-11

JESUS WAS BORN in the town of Bethlehem in Judaea, during the time when Herod was king. Soon afterwards, some men who studied the stars came from the east to Jerusalem and asked, "Where is the baby born to be the king of the Jews? We saw his star when it came up in the east and we have come to worship him." When King Herod heard about this, he was very upset, and so was everyone else in Jerusalem... He sent them to Bethlehem with these instructions: "Go and make a careful search for the child, and when you find him, let me know, so that I too may go and worship him." And so they left, and on their way they saw the same star they had seen in the east. When they saw it, how happy they were, what joy was theirs! It went ahead of them until it stopped over the place where the child was. They went into the house and when they saw the child with his mother Mary, they knelt down and worshipped him. They brought out their gifts of gold, frankincense, and myrrh, and presented them to him.

1. READING

What is going on?

Read the text and ask, what is going on? What strikes you about this passage? Details? Actions?

Possible prompts:

- Wise men from the east searching for the baby Jesus.
- They want to worship him.
- They ask for directions from a wicked man, King Herod.
- God guided them by a star.
- Finding Jesus they brought out their gifts of gold, frankincense and myrrh.

2. REFLECTION

What does it mean for us?

Read the text again. What phrase do you like in the text and why? What word attracts you? How does the text speak to you in the various places and situations you find yourself?

Possible prompts:

- What signs lead us to Jesus?
- How hard do we look for him in our lives?
- Have we been led astray by bad advice or wrong directions?
- The gift to Jesus of our worship.
- What gifts do we offer him?

3. RESPONSE

Making some prayers

Read the text again. We have heard God's Word and we have tried to see what it means. We can talk to Jesus about his message. It can be a prayer you know or one you make up.

Possible prompts:

- Thank you for your many gifts: life, love, family and friends.
- Give us the grace to keep searching.
- Thank you for letting us find you.
- What gift, Jesus, would you like from me?
- Help those who go astray in their lives and are lost.

4. REST

Enjoy the text

Read the text again.
Pause – a minute or two of silence with the text.
Invite pupils to take away a few words from this time of reflection, prayer or meditation as a message for today.

- Stay with the Magi at Bethlehem.
- Think of all the gifts we have.

A CONCLUDING PRAYER

We give you thanks
for all your gifts;
you live and reign forever and ever.

Amen.

Visit of Mary to Elizabeth

INTRODUCTION

■ *Scripture:* After the angel came to her, Mary set out to share the good news with her elderly cousin Elizabeth and to be with her in the final months of her pregnancy. The two mothers-to-be rejoice.

■ *Here I Am:* We have all been on visits to friends, family and different places and events. We also have all received visitors. Some are pleasant; others are strained and difficult. In this meditation we look at Mary's joyful visit to her cousin Elizabeth.

SCRIPTURE

Luke 1: 39-45

SOON AFTERWOODS Mary got ready and hurried off to a town in the hill-country of Judaea. She went into Zechariah's house and greeted Elizabeth. When Elizabeth heard Mary's greeting, the baby moved within her; Elizabeth was filled with the Holy Spirit and said in a loud voice. 'You are the most blessed of all women, and blessed is the child you will bear! Why should this great thing happen to me, that my Lord's mother comes to visit me? For as soon as I heard your greeting, the baby within me jumped with gladness. How happy you are to believe that the Lord's message to you will come true!"

1. READING

What is going on?

Read the text and ask, what is going on? What strikes you about this passage? Details? Actions?

Possible prompts:

- Mary hurrying off to visit her cousin Elizabeth.

- The effect of Mary's greeting.
- Elizabeth's greeting to Mary.
- Elizabeth is amazed that the Lord's mother comes to visit her.
- Elizabeth praises Mary's faith.

2. REFLECTION

What does it mean for us?

Read the text again. What phrase do you like in the text and why? What word attracts you? How does the text speak to you in the various places and situations you find yourself?

Possible prompts:

- Do we bring good news when we visit?
- Are our greetings sincere?
- How do we behave on visits?
- Has anyone ever praised our faith?

3. RESPONSE

Making some prayers

Read the text again. We have heard God's Word and we have tried to see what it means. We can talk to Jesus about his message. It can be a prayer you know or one you make up.

Possible prompts:

- Thank you, Lord, for your visits to us in sacraments, through friends and relatives.
- Thank you for all who visit our lives with good news.
- Give us generosity about family relationships and visits.
- May we be open to your Holy Spirit.
- May we be more like Mary.

4. REST

Enjoy the text

Read the text again.
Pause – a minute or two of silence with the text.
Invite pupils to take away a few words from this time of reflection, prayer or meditation as a message for today.

- Mary the most blessed of all women.
- Family love and demands.

A CONCLUDING PRAYER

Mary's Song

My soul glorifies the Lord,
my spirit rejoices in God, my Saviour.
He looks on his servant in her lowliness;
henceforth all ages will call me blessed.

The Almighty works marvels for me,
Holy his name!
His mercy is from age to age,
on those who fear him.

He puts forth his arm in strength
and scatters the proud-hearted.
He casts the mighty from their thrones
and raises the lowly.

He fills the starving with good things,
sends the rich away empty-handed.

He protects Israel, his servant,
remembering his mercy,
the mercy promised to our fathers,
to Abraham and his sons for ever.

Elijah on pilgrimage

INTRODUCTION

■ *Scripture*: About the year 860 BC the Prophet Elijah was engaged in a life and death struggle to defend the true worship of God against the cult of Baal, which was supported by the King's wife, Jezebel. After defeating the false prophets on Mount Carmel, Elijah, pursued by Jezebel is depressed and discouraged. God looks after him and he can go on pilgrimage to Mount Horeb, that is Sinai, where God had given the Law to Moses.

■ *Here I Am*: Journeys are part of our daily lives – some short, some long, some pleasant, some dangerous. Some journeys are memorable, others we forget very quickly. Life itself is a journey from the moment we are born until we enter our heavenly home. The Church refers to Mary's life as a "pilgrimage of faith" (LG 58). In this meditation we journey with Elijah and meet the Lord of all journeys.

SCRIPTURE

1 Kings 19: 1-5

KING AHAB told his wife Jezebel everything that Elijah had done and how he had put all the prophets of Baal to death. She sent a message to Elijah "May the gods strike me dead if by this time tomorrow I don't do the same thing to you that you did to the prophets." Elijah was afraid and fled for his life; he took his servant and went to Beersheba in Judah. Leaving the servant there, Elijah walked a whole day into the wilderness. He stopped and sat down in the shade of a tree and wished he would die. "It's too much, Lord," he prayed. "Take away my life; I might as well be dead!" He lay down under the tree and fell asleep. Suddenly an angel touched him and said, "Wake up and eat." He looked around, and saw a loaf of bread and a jar of water near his head. He ate and drank, and lay down again. The Lord's angel returned and woke him up a second time saying, "Get up and eat or the journey will be too much for you." Elijah got up, ate and drank, and the food gave him enough strength to walk forty days to Sinai, the holy mountain. There he went into a cave to spend the night.

1. READING

What is going on?

Read the text and ask, what is going on? What strikes you about this passage? Details? Actions?

Possible prompts:

- Elijah runs away from danger.
- Sitting under a tree he is weary, depressed and fearful.
- He wishes he were dead.
- God sends an angel to comfort and strengthen him with food.
- Elijah got up, ate and drank and journeyed across the desert to God's holy mountain.

2. REFLECTION

What does it mean for us?

Read the text again. What phrase do you like in the text and why? What word attracts you? How does the text speak to you in the various places and situations you find yourself?

Possible prompts:

- Have we felt like Elijah: lonely, fed up, afraid?
- Elijah told God about how he was feeling – that is the way we should pray.
- God heard Elijah's prayer and gave a surprising answer; have we had unexpected answers to prayer?
- God will give us enough help and strength for our journeys.

3. RESPONSE

Making some prayers

Read the text again. We have heard God's Word and we have tried to see what it means. We can talk to Jesus about his message. It can be a prayer you know or one you make up.

Possible prompts:

- Strengthen us when we grow sad or lonely.
- Help us to turn to you always, especially in time of danger and upset.
- Give your strength and support to all who are tired and weary.
- May all who are travelling have a safe journey.
- Guide and support all of us at all times.

4. REST

Enjoy the text

Read the text again.

Pause – a minute or two of silence with the text.

Invite pupils to take away a few words from this time of reflection, prayer or meditation as a message for today.

- Elijah fed up.
- God strengthens Elijah.

A CONCLUDING PRAYER

Angel of God, my guardian dear,
to whom God's love commits me here.
Ever this day/night be at my side
to light, to guard, to rule and guide.
Amen.

Seeing Jesus

INTRODUCTION

■ *Scripture*: Zacchaeus was a wealthy man and a tax collector, who was dishonest. Out of curiosity, he climbed a tree to catch a glimpse of Jesus. Jesus singles him out and Zacchaeus is changed forever.

■ *Here I Am:* We tend to categorise people according to their appearance, their ethnic group or race, their social condition, where they live. God does not look on us in this way. For God everybody is special – nobody is excluded. Jesus here gives a special invitation to a rich man who was despised because of his sin and dishonesty by those who thought of themselves as "good people".

SCRIPTURE

Luke 19: 1-10

JESUS WENT on into Jericho and was passing through. There was a chief tax collector there named Zacchaeus who was rich. He was trying to see who Jesus was, but he was a little man and could not see Jesus because of the crowd. So he ran ahead of the crowd and climbed a sycamore tree to see Jesus, who was going to pass that way. When Jesus came to that place, he looked up and said to Zacchaeus, "Hurry down, Zacchaeus, because I must stay in your house today." Zacchaeus hurried down and welcomed him with great joy. All the people who saw it started grumbling. "This man has gone as a guest to the home of a sinner!" Zacchaeus stood up and said to the Lord, "Listen sir, I will give half my belongings to the poor, and if I have cheated anyone, I will pay him back four times as much." Jesus said to him, "Salvation has come to this house today, for this man also, is a descendant of Abraham. The Son of Man came to seek and to save the lost."

1. READING

What is going on?

Read the text and ask, what is going on? What strikes you about this passage? Details? Actions?

Possible prompts:

- Zacchaeus the rich tax collector was curious and wanted to see Jesus.
- Tree-climbing is not adult behaviour!
- Jesus looks up at Zacchaeus and invites himself to a meal.
- The religious people grumble.
- Zacchaeus is converted.
- Jesus said he came to save the lost; those in need are special to Jesus.

2. REFLECTION

What does it mean for us?

Read the text again. What phrase do you like in the text and why? What word attracts you? How does the text speak to you in the various places and situations you find yourself?

Possible prompts:

- It can take an effort for us to see Jesus.
- We are special to Jesus.
- Other people, maybe ones we do not like, are special too.
- Meeting Jesus can change our lives.
- People will grumble at us sometimes when we are doing something good.
- Zacchaeus welcomed Jesus: can't we?

3. RESPONSE

Making some prayers

Read the text again. We have heard God's Word and we have tried to see what it means. We can talk to Jesus about his message. It can be a prayer you know or one you make up.

Possible prompts:

- May we be on the look-out to see you, Jesus.
- Jesus, you look on me too with special love.
- Jesus, may I see myself as you see me.
- Change me Lord... as you changed Zacchaeus.
- Help me not to condemn others.
- Forgive us our trespasses as we forgive those who trespass against us...

4. REST

Enjoy the text

Read the text again.
Pause – a minute or two of silence with the text.
Invite pupils to take away a few words from this time of reflection, prayer or meditation as a message for today.

- Zacchaeus looked for Jesus and found his real self.
- Jesus invites himself into our lives.
- I am special for God.

A CONCLUDING PRAYER

Jesus, I love and adore you
You are a special friend to me.
Welcome, dear Jesus, welcome.
Thank you for coming to us.

Traditional

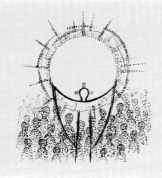

Jesus the student

INTRODUCTION

■ *Scripture:* Jesus grew up as an ordinary boy. He had to learn the Hebrew Scriptures. Ordinary people like his family did not have books, so students learned by memory, and by question and answer with the teacher.

■ *Here I Am*: As Christians we have important religious books like the bible, the books used in worship and the Church's Catechism. From them we learn our faith; we also have discussion with questions and answers from our teachers.

SCRIPTURE

Luke 2: 41-47, 51-52

EVERY YEAR the parents of Jesus went to Jerusalem for the Passover Festival. When Jesus was twelve years old, they went to the festival as usual. When the festival was over, they started back home, but the boy Jesus stayed in Jerusalem. His parents did not know this; they thought that he was with the group, so they travelled a whole day and then started looking for him among their relatives and friends. They did not find him, so they went back to Jerusalem looking for him. On the third day they found him in the Temple, sitting with the Jewish teachers, listening to them and asking questions. All who heard him were amazed at his intelligent answers… Jesus went back with them to Nazareth, where he was obedient to them. His mother treasured all these things in her heart. Jesus grew both in body and in wisdom, gaining favour with God and men.

1. READING

What is going on?

Read the text and ask, what is going on? What strikes you about this passage? Details? Actions?

Possible prompts:

- Jesus stayed in Jerusalem.
- Joseph and Mary were worried until they found him.
- He was in the Temple with the Jewish teachers.

40

- Listening to them and asking questions.
- All were amazed at his intelligent answers.
- Jesus grew up normally, becoming wise and strong.

2. REFLECTION

What does it mean for us?

Read the text again. What phrase do you like in the text and why? What word attracts you? How does the text speak to you in the various places and situations you find yourself?

Possible prompts:

- Religious classes are important.
- Knowing God's teaching and his will.
- Having respect for holy books, especially the bible.
- We also learn religion by questions and answers.
- Jesus went back with his parents and was obedient to them.
- He grew in body and wisdom.

3. RESPONSE

Making some prayers

Read the text again. We have heard God's Word and we have tried to see what it means. We can talk to Jesus about his message. It can be a prayer you know or one you make up.

Possible prompts:

- Teach me your ways.
- O Holy Spirit, give me a love for your scriptures.
- Speak, Lord, your servant is listening.
- Your Word is a lamp for my steps.
- Jesus, help me when obedience is hard.

4. REST

Enjoy the text

Read the text again.

Pause – a minute or two of silence with the text.

Invite pupils to take away a few words from this time of reflection, prayer or meditation as a message for today.

- Jesus the student.
- Love of learning about God.

A CONCLUDING PRAYER

From your throne of glory,
Send me your wisdom
That dwells with you,
To help and guide me.

Based on Wis 9: 10-11

Abraham's hospitality

INTRODUCTION

■ *Scripture*: Sometime around 1650 BC God called Abraham to leave his home at Ur, near the present Persian Gulf, and go to the Land of Promise. God instructed Abraham and gave him promises of many descendants. Abraham trusted God so strongly that he is called in the liturgy, "Our father in faith".

■ *Here I Am:* Lives are marked by key moments of happiness, joy and sorrow. Frequently these moments are celebrated in the Church or at home: baptism, birthdays, First Communion, confession, marriage, ordination, sacrament of the sick; others are celebrated at home like birthdays, anniversaries, homecomings, departures, visitors, death.

SCRIPTURE

Genesis 18: 1-18

THE LORD appeared to Abraham at the sacred trees of Mamre. As Abraham was sitting at the entrance of his tent during the hottest part of the day, he looked up and saw three men standing there. As soon as he saw them, he ran out to meet them. Bowing down with his face touching the ground, he said, "Sirs, please do not pass my home without stopping; I am here to serve you. Let me bring some water for you to wash your feet; you can rest here beneath this tree. I will also bring a bit of food; it will give you strength to continue your journey. You have honoured me by coming to my home, so let me serve you." They replied, "Thank you, we accept." Abraham hurried into the tent and said to Sarah, "Quick, take a sack of your best flour, and bake some bread." Then he ran to the herd and picked out a calf that was tender and fat, and gave it to a servant who hurried to get it ready. He took some cream, some milk, and the meat and set the food before the men. There under the tree he served them himself, and they ate.

1. READING

What is going on?

Read the text and ask, what is going on? What strikes you about this passage? Details? Actions?

Possible prompts:

- The Lord visits Abraham.

- Abraham ran out to welcome the three visitors.
- He offers hospitality – washing their feet.
- He is generous with his food – he wants to celebrate.
- The divine messengers accept the hospitality.

2. REFLECTION

What does it mean for us?

Read the text again. What phrase do you like in the text and why? What word attracts you? How does the text speak to you in the various places and situations you find yourself?

Possible prompts:

- The Lord comes to us in different people.
- How do we welcome Jesus who comes to us in others?
- Are we generous in hospitality?
- How do we celebrate other people's joys and sorrows?
- Celebrating God's presence in our lives.

3. RESPONSE

Making some prayers

Read the text again. We have heard God's Word and we have tried to see what it means. We can talk to Jesus about his message. It can be a prayer you know or one you make up.

Possible prompts:

- Open my eyes to see you in others.
- Make me generous with all the gifts you have given me.
- In celebrations help me to make other people feel good.
- Feed me with the food of your Word.
- Fill me with your Spirit.

4. REST

Enjoy the text

Read the text again.

Pause – a minute or two of silence with the text.

Invite pupils to take away a few words from this time of reflection, prayer or meditation as a message for today.

- Being welcoming.
- God coming in hidden ways.

A CONCLUDING PRAYER

Lord, I thank you for the occasions we have to celebrate.
May we also celebrate in your church the sacraments of your grace.
Keep us close to you until we reach the eternal celebration in your heavenly home. Amen.

The grateful leper

Here I Am: THANKSGIVING

INTRODUCTION

■ *Scripture:* Ancient peoples had a great fear of leprosy, which was contagious, that is, spread by contact. There was no cure then. Lepers were cut off from all people. Jesus cures ten lepers, but only one, a Samaritan outcast, says "thanks." He is given still greater blessings.

■ *Here I Am:* The sacraments use human symbols and appeal to our human experience. The greatest of them, Holy Communion and the Mass are acts of thanksgiving when we come before God along with Jesus to offer his sacrifice for the world and ourselves.

SCRIPTURE

Luke 17: 11-19

AS JESUS made his way to Jerusalem, he went along the border between Samaria and Galilee. He was going into a village when he was met by ten men suffering from a dreadful skin-disease. They stood at a distance and shouted, "Jesus! Master! Take pity on us!" Jesus saw them and said to them, "Go and let the priests examine you." On the way they were made clean. When one of them saw that he was healed, he came back, praising God in a loud voice. He threw himself to the ground at Jesus' feet and thanked him. The man was a Samaritan. Jesus said, "There were ten men who were healed; where are the other nine? Why is this foreigner the only one who came back to give thanks to God." And Jesus said to him, "Get up and go; your faith has made you well."

1. READING

What is going on?

Read the text and ask, what is going on? What strikes you about this passage? Details? Actions?

Possible prompts:

- Jesus meeting the lepers who had to keep their distance.
- In their hopeless state they appealed to Jesus.
- They had a skin-disease and stood at a distance and shouted for mercy or pity.
- Their delight in being healed.
- Only one man returned to express gratitude.

2. REFLECTION

What does it mean for us?

Read the text again. What phrase do you like in the text and why? What word attracts you? How does the text speak to you in the various places and situations you find yourself?

Possible prompts:

- Like the lepers, we need mercy.
- All we have to do is turn to God.
- Jesus is rich in mercy and raises us out of our selfishness and sin.
- Having a thankful heart opens us to joy and beauty.
- Thankfulness heals and changes us.
- Jesus welcomes all who are hurting in mind, body and spirit.

3. RESPONSE

Making some prayers

Read the text again. We have heard God's Word and we have tried to see what it means. We can talk to Jesus about his message. It can be a prayer you know or one you make up.

Possible prompts:

- Thank you Jesus for your love and forgiveness.
- Thank you for so many good things in my life.
- Thank you for your sacraments.
- Thank you for your Church where we can find your mercy and healing.
- Help me to be more positive and more grateful in the small things of life.

4. REST

Enjoy the text

Read the text again.

Pause – a minute or two of silence with the text.

Invite pupils to take away a few words from this time of reflection, prayer or meditation as a message for today.

- Jesus, have pity on us.
- The pain of ingratitude.

A CONCLUDING PRAYER

Lift up your hearts.
Let us give thanks to the Lord our God.
It is right to give God thanks and praise.

From the Liturgy

Memorial of the Lord

INTRODUCTION

■ *Scripture:* In St Paul we find some very important little summaries of the teaching he had received when he was converted to Christianity. Here we have his account of the Last Supper, when Jesus celebrated the first Eucharist and left it to the Church as a memorial.

■ *Here I Am:* Memories, particularly good memories, sustain us when a loved one leaves us or dies. In Jesus' case he goes and he remains. From the Last Supper he went out to die, then he rose and ascended into heaven, but he devised a way of remaining always with us. This is the Mass.

SCRIPTURE

1 Corinthians 11: 23-26

FOR I RECEIVED from the Lord the teaching that I passed on to you that the Lord Jesus, on the night he was betrayed, took a piece of bread, gave thanks to God, broke it, and said, "This is my body, which is for you. Do this in memory of me." In the same way, after the supper he took the cup and said, "This cup is God's new covenant, sealed with my blood. Whenever you drink it, do so in memory of me." This means that every time you eat this bread and drink from this cup you proclaim the Lord's death until he comes.

1. READING

What is going on?

Read the text and ask, what is going on? What strikes you about this passage? Details? Actions?

Possible prompts:

- The night Jesus was betrayed.
- Bread and wine.
- He took a piece of bread, gave thanks and broke it.
- This is my body, which is for you… the cup sealed in my blood.
- Do this in memory of me.
- We proclaim the Lord's death until he comes.

2. REFLECTION

What does it mean for us?

Read the text again. What phrase do you like in the text and why? What word attracts you? How does the text speak to you in the various places and situations you find yourself?

Possible prompts:

- Jesus gives us the gift of himself.
- Memorial of his death and resurrection.
- Jesus remaining with us.
- The wonder of the Mass.
- Jesus comes to us in Holy Communion.

3. RESPONSE

Making some prayers

Read the text again. We have heard God's Word and we have tried to see what it means. We can talk to Jesus about his message. It can be a prayer you know or one you make up.

Possible prompts:

- Christ has died, Christ is risen, Christ will come again.
- When we eat this bread and drink this cup, we proclaim your death, Lord Jesus, until you come in glory.
- Thank you for the gift of love and friendship in the Eucharist.
- Thank you for being present for us in the Blessed Sacrament.

4. REST

Enjoy the text

Read the text again. Pause – a minute or two of silence with the text. Invite pupils to take away a few words from this time of reflection, prayer or meditation as a message for today.

- Such generous love.
- A rich memorial.
- This is my body which is for you.

A CONCLUDING PRAYER

Lord, may I receive your gifts with purity of heart.
May they bring me healing and strength now and forever. Amen.

(From the Mass)

God feeds His people

INTRODUCTION

■ *Scripture*: The dramatic story of the feeding of five thousand with five loaves and a few fish recalls the way in which God fed his people in the desert with manna.

■ *Here I Am*: The miracle of the loaves shows Jesus caring for his people. It also looks forward to the still greater feeding through the Eucharist. The same words are used for both: "took, thanked, broke, gave."

SCRIPTURE

Luke 9: 10-17

THE APOSTLES came back and told Jesus everything they had done. He took them with him, and they went off by themselves to a town called Bethsaida. When the crowds heard about it, they followed him. He welcomed them, spoke to them about the Kingdom of God, and healed those who needed it. When the sun was beginning to set, the twelve disciples came to him and said, "Send the people away so that they can go to the villages and farms around here and find food and lodging because this is a lonely place." But Jesus said to them, "You yourselves give them something to eat." They answered, "All we have are five loaves and two fish. Do you want us to go and buy food for this whole crowd?" (There were about five thousand men there.) Jesus said to his disciples "Make the people sit down in groups of about fifty each." After the disciples had done so, Jesus took the five loaves and two fish, looked up to heaven, thanked God for them, broke them, gave them to the disciples to distribute to the people. They all ate and had enough, and the disciples took up twelve baskets of what was left over.

1. READING

What is going on?

Read the text and ask, what is going on? What strikes you about this passage? Details? Actions?

Possible prompts:

- The crowd followed Jesus.
- The twelve apostles wanted to send the people away as it was late.
- Jesus told them to feed the crowd.
- Only five loaves and two fish.
- The picnic: Jesus told the people to sit in groups of fifty.
- He fed them.
- Nobody was hungry.

2. REFLECTION

What does it mean for us?

Read the text again. What phrase do you like in the text and why? What word attracts you? How does the text speak to you in the various places and situations you find yourself?

Possible prompts:

- It would have been lovely to have been at Jesus' picnic.
- It was those who followed him who were fed.
- I am fed by Jesus in Holy Communion.
- It is in this Holy Sacrament that we get the strength we need.
- We, too, are taken, blessed, broken and given for others.
- The wonder of it all!

3. RESPONSE

Making some prayers.

Read the text again. We have heard God's Word and we have tried to see what it means. We can talk to Jesus about his message. It can be a prayer you know or one you make up.

Possible prompts:

- Bring us closer to you.
- Strengthen and heal us.
- Feed all who hunger and thirst for you.
- You are the Bread of Life.
- Feed us with the food that will last.

4. REST

Enjoy the text

Read the text again.
Pause – a minute or two of silence with the text.
Invite pupils to take away a few words from this time of reflection, prayer or meditation as a message for today.

- God feeds his people.
- The concern of Jesus.
- Take, bless, break, give.

A CONCLUDING PRAYER

*Christ has no body
  now on earth
  but yours:
No hands
  but yours:
No feet
  but yours:
Yours are the eyes
  through which I must
  look with Christ's compassion on
  the world.
Yours are the feet
  with which he is to go about
  doing good.
Yours are the hands
  with which he is to bless mankind now.*

St Teresa of Avila

49

Emmaus

INTRODUCTION

■ *Scripture:* Two disciples of Jesus are sad because Jesus has died. They meet a stranger, who turns out to be Jesus. He opens the scriptures for them. They recognise him in the breaking of the Bread.

■ *Here I Am:* We meet Jesus in the same way as the two disciples on the road to Emmaus: by being open to the stranger; by having the scriptures explained to us; in the breaking of the Bread.

SCRIPTURE

Luke 24: 13-20, 25-32

ON THAT SAME DAY two of Jesus' followers were going to a village named Emmaus, about eleven kilometres from Jerusalem, and they were talking to each other about all the things that had happened. As they talked and discussed, Jesus himself drew near and walked along with them; they saw him, but somehow did not recognise him. Jesus said to them, "What are you talking about to each other, as you walk along?" They stood still, with sad faces. One of them, named Cleopas, asked him, "Are you the only visitor in Jerusalem who doesn't know the things that have been happening these last few days?" "What things," he asked. "The things that happened to Jesus of Nazareth," they answered. "This man was a prophet and was considered by God and by all the people to be powerful in everything he said and did. Our chief priests and rulers handed him over to be sentenced to death, and he was crucified... Then Jesus said to them, "How foolish you are, how slow you are to believe everything the prophets said! Was it not necessary for the Messiah to suffer these things and then to enter his glory?" And Jesus explained to them what was said about himself in all the Scriptures, beginning with the books of Moses and the writings of all the prophets. As they came near the village to which they were going, Jesus acted as if he were going farther; but they held him back, saying, "Stay with us; the day is almost over and it is getting dark." So he went in to stay with them. He sat down to eat with them, took the bread and said the blessing, then he broke the bread and gave it to them. Then their eyes were opened and they recognised him, but he disappeared from their sight. They said to each other, "Wasn't it like a fire burning in us when he talked to us on the road and explained the Scriptures to us?"

1. READING

What is going on?

Read the text and ask, what is going on? What strikes you about this passage? Details? Actions?

Possible prompts:

- Two disciples going to Emmaus.
- Jesus joined them on the way but they did not recognise him.
- They told Jesus why they were sad.
- He explained to them what was written about him in Scriptures.
- They invited Jesus to stay with them.
- They recognised him in the breaking of bread.

2. REFLECTION

What does it mean for us?

Read the text again. What phrase do you like in the text and why? What word attracts you? How does the text speak to you in the various places and situations you find yourself?

Possible prompts:

- How can we recognise Jesus?
- Can we welcome Jesus in others?
- We need the help of Jesus or the Holy Spirit to grasp the meaning of the scriptures.
- Jesus comes to us in the Eucharist.
- We can tell others the Good News about Jesus.

3. RESPONSE

Making some prayers

Read the text again. We have heard God's Word and we have tried to see what it means. We can talk to Jesus about his message. It can be a prayer you know or one you make up.

Possible prompts:

- Walk beside us this day and always.
- Open our eyes to see you, our ears to hear you, our hearts to love you.
- Help us welcome you today in others.
- Make us strong to proclaim your Good News.

4. REST

Enjoy the text

Read the text again. Pause - a minute or two of silence with the text. Invite pupils to take away a few words from this time of reflection, prayer or meditation as a message for today.

- Jesus walks unrecognised.
- He opens our eyes.
- Stay with us.

A CONCLUDING PRAYER

Christ has died,
Christ is risen,
Christ will come again.

Gethsemane

INTRODUCTION

■ *Scripture*: After the Last Supper Jesus went off to pray about the terrible ordeal which lay before him. His disciples were no help: they slept. Eventually, with the Father's help, Jesus pulled himself around to give his life to save us all.

■ *Here I Am*: It can be very hard to give things away. It is much harder to give our time, our talents, or our personal gifts to others. The hardest of all is to give ourselves when we think totally about others. In this, as in everything else, Jesus is our model. Here he struggles before he can give himself for us on the Cross.

SCRIPTURE

Luke 22: 39-46

JESUS LEFT THE CITY and went, as he usually did, to the Mount of Olives; and the disciples went with him. When he arrived at the place, he said to them, "Pray that you will not fall into temptation." Then he went off from them about the distance of a stone's throw and knelt down and prayed. "Father," he said, "if you will, take this cup of suffering away from me. Not my will, however, but your will be done." An angel from heaven appeared to him and strengthened him. In great anguish he prayed even more fervently, his sweat was like drops of blood falling to the ground. Rising from his prayer, he went back to the disciples, and found them asleep, worn out by their grief. He said to them, "Why are you sleeping? Get up and pray that you will not fall into temptation."

1. READING

What is going on?

Read the text and ask, what is going on? What strikes you about this passage? Details? Actions?

Possible prompts:

- Jesus' distress, his agony in the garden.
- His prayer.
- He gives himself for us.
- An angel comes to strengthen Jesus.
- His sweat becomes like drops of blood.
- Rising from prayer he finds his disciples fast asleep.

2. REFLECTION

What does it mean for us?

Read the text again. What phrase do you like in the text and why? What word attracts you? How does the text speak to you in the various places and situations you find yourself?

Possible prompts:

- Such love for us on the part of Jesus.
- Jesus in distress prays to the Father; when troubled we are to do the same.
- We need help to be generous in giving ourselves.
- Jesus warns: "Get up and pray that you will not fall into temptation."

3. RESPONSE

Making some prayers

Read the text again. We have heard God's Word and we have tried to see what it means. We can talk to Jesus about his message. It can be a prayer you know or one you make up.

Possible prompts:

- Forgive us when we give in to temptation.
- Teach us to pray for strength not to give in.
- Bless our family, our teachers, and our friends who give themselves for us.
- Protect those who risk their lives for others.
- Help us to see your will.
- Thank you, Lord, for laying down your life for love of me.

4. REST

Enjoy the text

Read the text again.

Pause – a minute or two of silence with the text.

Invite pupils to take away a few words from this time of reflection, prayer or meditation as a message for today.

- The struggle of Jesus.
- Jesus gave himself for us.

A CONCLUDING PRAYER

Teach us, good Lord, to serve as you deserve,
to give and not to count the cost,
to fight and not to heed the wounds,
to toil and not to seek for rest,
to labour and not to ask for any reward
save that of knowing I do your will;
through Jesus Christ our Lord.

St Ignatius Loyola

Calvary

INTRODUCTION

■ *Scripture*: The stark scene on Calvary as the Messiah, the Son of God, is crucified. The apparently small details have significance in allowing us to grasp the meaning of this central act in the history of the world.

■ *Here I Am*: Continuing the Lenten journey we look to its climax on Calvary. Mary is there and the Beloved Disciple, who represents us; both stood at the foot of the Cross united in the pain of the event.

SCRIPTURE

John 19: 23-30

AFTER THE SOLDIERS had crucified Jesus, they took his clothes and divided them into four parts, one part for each soldier. They also took the robe, which was made of one piece of woven cloth without any seams in it. The soldiers said to one another, "Let's not tear it, let's throw dice to see who will get it." This happened in order to make the scripture come true: "They divided my clothes among themselves and gambled for my robe." And this is what the soldiers did. Standing close to Jesus' cross were his mother, his mother's sister, Mary the wife of Clopas, and Mary Magdalene. Jesus saw his mother and the disciple he loved standing there; so he said to his mother, "Here is your son." Then he said to the disciple, "She is your mother." From that time the disciple took her to live in his home. Jesus knew that by now everything had been completed; and in order to make the scripture come true, he said, "I am thirsty." A bowl was there, full of cheap wine; so a sponge was soaked in the wine, put on a stalk of hyssop, and lifted up to his lips. Jesus drank the wine and said, "It is finished!" Then he bowed his head and died.

1. READING

What is going on?

Read the text and ask, what is going on? What strikes you about this passage? Details? Actions?

Possible prompts:

- The horror of crucifixion.
- The soldiers gambled for his clothes.
- Jesus gave the Beloved Disciple to his Mother Mary, and gave Mary to him.
- Jesus wanted all Scriptures to come true, so he said; "I am thirsty."
- Jesus drank the wine and said, "It is finished." He bowed his head and died.

2. REFLECTION

What does it mean for us?

Read the text again. What phrase do you like in the text and why? What word attracts you? How does the text speak to you in the various places and situations you find yourself?

Possible prompts:

- The love that brought Jesus to die for us.
- The soldiers uncaring – gambling for a few clothes. Would we?
- We can join with Mary in her pain.
- Mary became our Mother at Calvary.
- Perhaps I should look more carefully at the crucifix: it is a symbol of love.

3. RESPONSE

Making some prayers

Read the text again. We have heard God's Word and we have tried to see what it means. We can talk to Jesus about his message. It can be a prayer you know or one you make up.

Possible prompts:

- Thank you Jesus for dying for us.
- Thank you for giving us, Mary, as our Mother.
- Jesus, help us to be strong when pain, disappointments or fears come our way.
- Be close to all who will die today.

4. REST

Enjoy the text

Read the text again.
Pause – a minute or two of silence with the text.
Invite pupils to take away a few words from this time of reflection, prayer or meditation as a message for today.

- The crucifix.
- Jesus' love and courage.

A CONCLUDING PRAYER

We adore you, O Christ,
and we praise you
because by your Holy Cross
you have redeemed the world.

(From the Liturgy)

Temptation of Jesus

INTRODUCTION

■ *Scripture*: At the beginning of his public ministry of preaching and healing, just after his baptism, Jesus goes away for a long period of prayer in the remote desert. There Satan tempts him to avoid the Father's plan, which was that he die for our sins. Satan tempts him with popularity, power, and idolatry. Jesus dismisses each temptation with a phrase from Scripture.

■ *Here I Am*: We are continually faced by choices: to buy one bar of sweets or another, to watch one programme or another, to go out or stay in. Most of these choices do not matter much; they are neutral; they do not make us a better or worse person. But there are other choices that are between good and evil. Then it is important that we choose rightly. But sometimes the choice is not too clear. Satan dresses up as good the temptations he places before Jesus.

SCRIPTURE

Matthew 4: 1-11

THEN THE SPIRIT led Jesus into the desert to be tempted by the Devil. After spending forty days and nights without food, Jesus was hungry. Then the Devil came to him and said, "if you are God's Son, order these stones to turn into bread." But Jesus answered, "The scripture says, 'Man cannot live on bread alone, but needs every word that God speaks.' " Then the Devil took Jesus to Jerusalem, the Holy City, set him on the highest point of the Temple, and said to him, "If you are God's Son, throw yourself down, for the scripture says, 'God will give orders to his angels about you; they will hold you up with their hands, so that not even your feet will be hurt on the stones.' " Jesus answered, "But the scripture also says, 'Do not put the Lord your God to the test.' " Then the Devil took Jesus to a very high mountain and showed him all the kingdoms of the world in all their greatness. "All this I will give you," the Devil said, "if you kneel down and worship me."

Then Jesus answered, "Go away, Satan! The scripture says, 'Worship the Lord your God and serve only him!' " Then the Devil left Jesus; and the angels came and helped him.

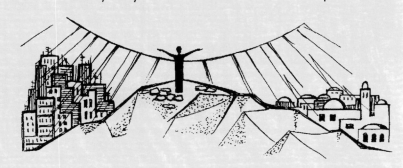

1. READING

What is going on?

Read the text and ask, what is going on? What strikes you about this passage? Details? Actions?

Possible prompts:

- After forty days without food Jesus was hungry.
- The temptation to be a dramatic miracle worker for his own good.
- The temptation to be a spectacular figure – flying through the air.
- The temptation to follow Satan's ways.
- Jesus is strong against each temptation.
- He follows the will of his Father.

2. REFLECTION

What does it mean for us?

Read the text again. What phrase do you like in the text and why? What word attracts you? How does the text speak to you in the various places and situations you find yourself?

Possible prompts:

- We are tempted when we are feeling weak or isolated.
- We can be tempted to look for an easy way out.
- Sometimes God wants something simple from us, not a big or dramatic act.
- It is easy to be taken in by false promises.
- In temptation we should turn to God, to his Word.

3. RESPONSE

Making some prayers

Read the text again. We have heard God's Word and we have tried to see what it means. We can talk to Jesus about his message. It can be a prayer you know or one you make up.

Possible prompts:

- Lord have mercy.
- Jesus be with me when I am tempted by evil.
- Help me to make the right choices.
- You are the Bread of Life.
- My Lord and my God.
- You are the Way, the Truth, and the Life.

4. REST

Enjoy the text

Read the text again.

Pause – a minute or two of silence with the text.

Invite pupils to take away a few yards from this time of reflection, prayer or meditation as a message for today.

- Lead us not into temptation.
- Worship God alone.

A CONCLUDING PRAYER

Deliver us from every evil
And grant us peace in our day.
In your mercy keep us free from sin.
And protect us from all anxiety.

(From the Liturgy)

Bearing fruit

INTRODUCTION

■ *Scripture*: The fig-tree and the vine are biblical symbols for God's people.
He cares for them, like a good gardener. But he expects fruit. Here the people have had three years to give fruit, that is, to accept the message of Jesus; they are on their last chance. We too need to have God's fruits showing in our lives.

■ *Here I Am*: Each day of each season we observe shrubs, flowers in bloom. People also delight in the growth of children. We grow, too, gradually or quickly in our love of God and each other; we can be selfish and refuse growth. Growing as a loving person can be difficult. We now listen to Jesus speak to us about growing.

SCRIPTURE

Luke 12: 6-9

THEN JESUS TOLD THEM this parable: "There was once a man who had a fig-tree growing in his vineyard.
He went looking for figs on it but found none.
So he said to his gardener, 'Look, for three years I have been coming here looking for figs on this fig-tree, and I haven't found any. Cut it down! Why should it go on using up the soil?' But the gardener answered, 'Leave it alone, sir, just one more year; I will dig round it and put in some manure. Then if the tree bears figs next year, so much the better; if not, then you can have it cut down.' "

1. READING

What is going on?

Read the text and ask, what is going on? What strikes you about this passage? Details? Actions?

Possible prompts:

- A man had a fig-tree growing in his vineyard.

- For three years disappointment: no fruit.
- The gardener asks for the tree to be given another chance, a year more.
- The gardener will help it to grow.

2. REFLECTION

What does it mean for us?

Read the text again. What phrase do you like in the text and why? What word attracts you? How does the text speak to you in the various places and situations you find yourself?

Possible prompts:

- We have been well looked after by Jesus, the gardener.
- What does Jesus the gardener find when he looks at us?
- Are we bearing the sort of fruit he likes: love, joy, peace, kindness, forgiveness?
- How does Jesus want us to grow?
- Jesus gives us another chance; how do we use it?

3. RESPONSE

Making some prayers

Read the text again. We have heard God's Word and we have tried to see what it means. We can talk to Jesus about his message. It can be a prayer you know or one you make up.

Possible prompts:

- Lord, help us to live and grow in your love.
- Be close to all who are tired and weary, to those who lose heart.
- Show us the fruit you expect from us at this time.
- Thank you for your patient forgiveness.
- Bless all gardeners and those who grow fruit for us.

4. REST

Enjoy the text

Read the text again.

Pause – a minute or two of silence with the text.

Invite pupils to take away a few words from this time of reflection, prayer or meditation as a message for today.

A fig-tree bending with fruit.
Jesus calls on us to grow in goodness.

A CONCLUDING PRAYER

Father in heaven,
* you have given us*
*   a mind to know you,*
*   a will to serve you,*
*   and a heart to love you.*
Be with us today in all that we do,
So that your light may shine out in
* our lives;*
through Jesus Christ our Lord.

St Thomas More

The Good Samaritan

INTRODUCTION

■ *Scripture*: After Jesus had told the rabbi that the law was in two commandments, the man further asked about the neighbour. Jesus takes the opportunity of widening Old Testament categories about love and neighbour and turns the knife in making the good person a Samaritan, one despised by the Jews.

■ *Here I Am*: Neighbours are people who live close by. Good neighbours are helpful. Jesus extends the word "neighbour" to all humanity. Everyone knows the phrase, "The Good Samaritan," from the chief character in the parable.

SCRIPTURE

Luke 10: 29-37

BUT THE TEACHER of the Law wanted to justify himself. So he asked Jesus, "Who is my neighbour." Jesus answered, "There was once a man who was going down from Jerusalem to Jericho when robbers attacked him, stripped him and beat him up, leaving him half dead. It so happened that a priest was going down that road; but when he saw the man, he walked on by, on the other side. In the same way a Levite also came along, went over and looked at the man, and them walked on by, on the other side. But a Samaritan who was travelling the way came upon the man, and when he saw him, his heart was filled with pity. He went over to him, poured oil and wine on his wounds and bandaged them, then he put the man on his own animal and took him to an inn, where he took care of him. The next day he took out two silver coins and gave them to the innkeeper. 'Take care of him,' He told the innkeeper, 'and when I come back this way, I will pay you whatever

else you spend on him.' "
And Jesus concluded, "in your opinion, which one of theses three acted like a neighbour towards the man attacked by the robbers?" The teacher of the Law answered, "The one who was kind to him." Jesus replied, "You go, then, and do the same."

60

1. READING

What is going on?

Read the text and ask, what is going on? What strikes you about this passage? Details? Actions?

Possible prompts:

- The characters in the text:
    - * Jesus,
    - * the teacher of the law,
    - * the robbers,
    - * the Levite and the priest,
    - * the Good Samaritan,
    - * the inn-keeper.
- Who is the neighbour?
- "You go and do the same."

2. REFLECTION

What does it mean for us?

Read the text again. What phrase do you like in the text and why? What word attracts you? How does the text speak to you in the various places and situations you find yourself?

Possible prompts:

- What kind of neighbour are we?
  Are we like the priest, the Levite or the Samaritan?
- Many people are not willing to stop and offer help.
- It is easy to be kind to the people we know and like.
- What would be a safe way of acting like the Good Samaritan today?

3. RESPONSE

Making some prayers

Read the text again. We have heard God's Word and we have tried to see what it means. We can talk to Jesus about his message. It can be a prayer you know or one you make up.

Possible prompts:

- Give us courage to reach out to the needy whoever they may be.
- Free us from selfishness.
- Protect us from racist ideas or speech.
- Thank you Lord for good neighbours.
- We pray for the Samaritans' organisation that does so much good.

4. REST

Enjoy the text

Read the text again.

Pause – a minute or two of silence with the text.

Invite pupils to take away a few words from this time of reflection, prayer or meditation as a message for today.

- Who is my neighbour?
- You go and do the same.

A CONCLUDING PRAYER

*God grant me the serenity
to accept the things I cannot change,
Courage to change the things I can
And wisdom to know the difference.*

Sharing

INTRODUCTION

■ *Scripture*: Jesus tells us that his kingdom is a great treasure. In the Apostles' Creed we profess our faith in the Communion of Saints. This is a sharing between good people alive and departed, as well as a sharing of the gifts God has given to his Church.

■ *Here I Am*: People treasure the strangest things: they can be costly and valuable like diamonds and great paintings, or apparently worthless, like rusty nails and seashells, except to the owner. Often what is a treasure to one person is quite ordinary to others. For us who are baptised in Christ our personal and precious treasure is Jesus and his Kingdom and the gifts we find in it.

SCRIPTURE

Matthew 13: 44-45

JESUS TAUGHT. "The Kingdom of heaven is like this. A man happens to find a treasure hidden in a field. He covers it up again, and is so happy that he goes and sells everything he has, and then goes back and buys that field."

1. READING

What is going on?

Read the text and ask, what is going on? What strikes you about this passage? Details? Actions?

Possible prompts:

- Stumbling on a treasure.
- Nobody must know.

- The excitement of the man.
- He gives up everything to buy the field.
- Nothing distracts this man from his hidden treasure.
- Jesus can give great truths with few words.

2. REFLECTION

What does it mean for us?

Read the text again. What phrase do you like in the text and why? What word attracts you? How does the text speak to you in the various places and situations you find yourself?

Possible prompts:

- Where is our treasure?
- What is our heart's desire?
- The friendship of the saints is a great treasure.
- The sacraments are immense treasures.
- Are we ever excited about our faith?
- People have at times to give up a lot for their beliefs.

3. RESPONSE

Making some prayers

Read the text again. We have heard God's Word and we have tried to see what it means. We can talk to Jesus about his message. It can be a prayer you know or one you make up.

Possible prompts:

- Thank you that we can share in our family of saints and holy people.
- We would like to be inspired by the example of the saints.
- Give us courage to seek you alone, Lord.
- Lord, you are our hidden treasure.
- Help us to seek genuine and lasting treasures.
- Deepen our appreciation of your sacraments and of your grace.

4. REST

Enjoy the text

Read the text again.

Pause – a minute or two of silence with the text.

Invite pupils to take away a few words from this time of reflection, prayer or meditation as a message for today.

- Where my treasure is...
- My heart's desire.

A CONCLUDING PRAYER

*Unfold for us
    the treasures of your Love;
Draw us into your family,
Father, Son and Holy Spirit.*

Moses is called

INTRODUCTION

■ *Scripture*: Around the year 1250 God's people were being oppressed in Egypt. Moses was a shepherd chosen by God to set his people free. But God had to form them in the desert, teaching them his way.

■ *Here I Am*: Special places are usually marked by experiences of special encounters such as love, beauty, friendship. These may be chance meetings; planned events or surprise unforgettable moments. A meeting with God will surely make a place special forever.

SCRIPTURE

Exodus 3: 1-8

ONE DAY while Moses was taking care of the sheep and goats of his father-in-law Jethro, the priest of Midian, he led the flock across the desert and came to Sinai, the holy mountain. There the angel of the Lord appeared to him as a flame coming from the middle of a bush. Moses saw that the bush was on fire but that it was not burning up. "This is strange," he thought, "Why isn't the bush burning up? I will go closer and see." When the Lord saw that Moses was coming closer, he called to him from the middle of the bush and said, "Moses! Moses!" He answered, "Yes, here I am." God said, "Do not come any closer. Take off your sandals, because you are standing on holy ground. I am the God of your ancestors, the God of Abraham, Isaac, and Jacob." So Moses covered his face, because he was afraid to look at God. Then the Lord said, "I have seen how cruelly my people are being treated in Egypt, I have heard them cry out to be rescued from their slave-drivers. I know all about their sufferings, and so I have come down to rescue them from the Egyptians and to bring them out of Egypt to a spacious land one which is rich and fertile."

1. READING

What is going on?

Read the text and ask, what is going on? What strikes you about this passage? Details? Actions?

Possible prompts:

- A flame from the middle of a bush.
- Moses is curious.
- He is told that he is standing on holy ground.
- I am the God of Abraham, Isaac and Jacob.
- Moses is afraid.
- God had been looking at his people's hardship and he will rescue them.

2. REFLECTION

What does it mean for us?

Read the text again. What phrase do you like in the text and why? What word attracts you? How does the text speak to you in the various places and situations you find yourself?

Possible prompts:

- When have we been aware of God's presence?
- Are there places where we feel God is close?
- Why would we be afraid of God?
- God is always willing to save us.
- We share with Jews and Moslems a belief in the God of Abraham.

3. RESPONSE

Making some prayers

Read the text again. We have heard God's Word and we have tried to see what it means. We can talk to Jesus about his message. It can be a prayer you know or one you make up.

Possible prompts:

- Thank you for special holy places.
- Help us to respect your holy places.
- You are the God of surprises.
- Thank you for saving us.
- We can find you, Lord, anywhere and everywhere.

4. REST

Enjoy the text

Read the text again.

Pause – a minute or two of silence with the text.

Invite pupils to take away a few words from this time of reflection, prayer or meditation as a message for today.

- Holy ground.
- Meeting God's love.

A CONCLUDING PRAYER

Visit this place we pray you, Lord.
Drive far away from it all the snares of
*   the enemy.*
May your holy angels stay here and guard
*   us in peace.*
And let your blessing be always upon us.
Through Christ our Lord.

Night Prayer of the Liturgy

God's ways

INTRODUCTION

■ *Scripture*: The Pharisees at the time of Jesus were rather legalistic; they thought of earning God's favour. In particular they were very exact about the Law, so that they would be right with God. Jesus taught that salvation is not earned, but is a free gift of God. We have no right to begrudge others the gifts they have received.

■ *Here I Am*: Our world and Church are marked by the wonder, pain and beauty of difference. There are different climates, different landscapes, different cultures, different foods, and different people with different ideas. But God has another way of looking at our differences – one marked by sheer generosity.

SCRIPTURE

Matthew 20: 1-16

THE KING OF HEAVEN is like this. Once there was a man who went out early in the morning to hire some men to work in his vineyard. He agreed to give them the regular wage, a silver coin a day, and sent them to work in his vineyard. Then he went out again to the market-place at eleven o'clock and saw some men standing there doing nothing, so he told them, "You men go and work in the vineyard, and I will pay you a fair wage." So they went! Then at twelve o'clock and again at three o'clock he did the same thing. It was nearly five o'clock when he went to the marketplace and saw some other men still standing there. Why are you wasting the whole day here doing nothing?" he asked them. "No one hired us" they answered. "Well, then, you also go and work in the vineyard," he told them.

When evening came, the owner told his foreman, "Call the workers and pay them their wages, starting with those who were hired last and ending with those who were hired first." The men who had begun to work at five o'clock were paid a silver coin each. So when the men who were the first to be hired came to be paid, they thought they would get more; but they too were given a silver coin each. They took their money and started grumbling against the employer. "These men who were hired last worked only one hour," they said, "while we put up with a whole day's work in the hot sun – yet you paid them the same as you paid us!" "Listen, friend," the owner answered one of them, "I have not cheated you. After all, you agreed to do a day's work for one silver coin. Now take your pay and go home. I want to give this man who was hired last as much as I have given you. Don't I have the right to do as I wish with my own money? Or are you jealous because I am generous." And Jesus concluded, "So those who are last will be first, and those who are first will be last."

1. READING

What is going on?

Read the text and ask, what is going on? What strikes you about this passage? Details? Actions?

Possible prompts:

- The owner of the vineyard hires people at different times of the day.
- Some people work all day, some as little as an hour.
- Some don't seem over-eager for work: they are not very early at the market-place.
- All paid the same.
- Some see it as unfair.
- The master is fair to all, but more generous to some.
- "Those who are last will be first, and those who are first will be last."

2. REFLECTION

What does it mean for us?

Read the text again. What phrase do you like in the text and why? What word attracts you? How does the text speak to you in the various places and situations you find yourself?

Possible prompts:

- It is good to be chosen and be treated fairly.
- Some seem to have more than others.
- We are not to be jealous, but give thanks for what we have.
- Am I eager to serve, laid back, or even lazy?
- Do I begrudge others?

3. RESPONSE

Making some prayers

Read the text again. We have heard God's Word and we have tried to see what it means. We can talk to Jesus about his message. It can be a prayer you know or one you make up.

Possible prompts:

- Lord, you love us as we are, thank you, Lord.
- Thank you for what we have received; we did not really earn it.
- Heal those who are bitter in heart.
- Bless all who are unemployed.
- Help all employers to be just and fair.

4. REST

Enjoy the text

Read the text again.

Pause – a minute or two of silence with the text.

Invite pupils to take away a few words from this time of reflection, prayer or meditation as a message for today.

- Are you jealous because I am generous?
- Contentment with what we have.

A CONCLUDING PRAYER

We give you thanks for all your gifts
*   that we have received,*
through Christ our Lord. Amen.

Final word

INTRODUCTION

■ *Scripture*: People at the time of Jesus – and since – have had a choice put before them: to be disciples or not. Some begin right with a big "yes" to God; others begin badly, but eventually do God's will. The parable can be read as religious history – the Jews and Jesus, or as our own personal history. The key is "final choice?" as in the quiz game.

■ *Here I Am*: By sin we say "no" to God our Father. But we can later repent and then do God's will. It is more foolish to say first a "yes" and then fail to follow through. It is how we end up that is important, that is, in repentance.

SCRIPTURE

Matthew 21: 28-31

JESUS SAID, "Now, what do you think? There was once a man who had two sons. He went to the elder one and said, 'Son, go and work in the vineyard today.' 'I don't want to,' he answered, but later he changed his mind and went. Then the father went to the other son and said the same thing. 'Yes, sir,' he answered, but he did not go. Which one of the two did what his father wanted?" "The elder one," they answered.

1. READING

What is going on?

Read the text and ask, what is going on? What strikes you about this passage? Details? Actions?

Possible prompts:

- Different choices in this parable.
- The first son seems a bit stubborn but is more loyal and dependable.
- The second son is two-faced.
- Both sons are flawed, but the first repents.
- The sense of duty of the elder son.

2. REFLECTION

What does it mean for us?

Read the text again. What phrase do you like in the text and why? What word attracts you? How does the text speak to you in the various places and situations you find yourself?

Possible prompts:

- What is our first instinct when asked to do something, "Yes" or "No"?
- We have all sometimes been like the first son, saying "no", then changing our minds.
- We have all been like the first second son, saying "yes" and then letting God or others down.
- Pride can hold us back from changing our mind.
- We rarely regret being generous and obedient.

3. RESPONSE

Making some prayers

Read the text again. We have heard God's Word and we have tried to see what it means. We can talk to Jesus about his message. It can be a prayer you know or one you make up.

Possible prompts:

- Help us to make good choices.
- Lord, we need your strength to follow through.
- It is hard, Lord, to have to climb down!
- Lord, let us listen to your Holy Spirit rather than to selfish feelings.
- Lord, help those who find work places difficult.

4. REST

Enjoy the text

Read the text again.

Pause – a minute or two of silence with the text.

Invite pupils to take away a few words from this time of reflection, prayer or meditation as a message for today.

- When we say, "yes"...
- When we say, "no"...

A CONCLUDING PRAYER

DEUT. 33:11

Direct, we ask you, O Lord,
All our actions by your holy inspiration
And carry them on by your gracious
*   assistance*
That every prayer and work of ours may
*   begin always with you*
And by you be happily ended.
Through Christ our Lord. Amen.

Paul's conversion

INTRODUCTION

■ *Scripture*: The conversion of Saul, who would later be called Paul, has entered our language. We speak of a "Damascus Road" experience. Paul the persecutor is made an apostle. The Christian community in the person of Ananias receives the enemy of the Church into its family.

■ *Here I Am*: We notice seasonal changes which happen gradually and yet startle us, e.g. in Spring suddenly all the leaves are green; Autumn sparkles with its reds, gold and orange. In our spiritual journey there can be highpoints, or sudden changes. But most change and healing are probably gradual though God's constant means of grace, like the sacrament of reconciliation.

SCRIPTURE

Acts 9: 1-8, 10-11, 17-19

IN THE MEANTIME Saul kept up his violent threats of murder against the followers of the Lord, He went to the High Priest and asked for letters of introduction to the synagogues in Damascus, so that if he should find there any followers of the Way of the Lord, he would be able to arrest them, both men and women, and bring them back to Jerusalem. As Saul was coming near the city of Damascus, suddenly a light from the sky flashed round him. He fell to the ground and heard a voice saying to him, "Saul, Saul! Why do you persecute me?" "Who are you, Lord?" he asked. "I am Jesus, whom you persecute," the voice said. "But get up and go into the city, where you will be told what you must do." The men who were travelling with Saul had stopped, not saying a word; they heard the voice but could not see anyone. Saul got up from the ground and opened his eyes, but could not see a thing. So they took him by the hand and led him into Damascus... There was a Christian in Damascus named Ananias. He had a vision in which the Lord said to him, "Ananias!" "Here I am Lord," he answered. The Lord said to him, "Get ready and go to Straight Street, and at the house of Judas ask for a man from Tarsus named Saul"... So Ananias went, entered the house where Saul was, and placed his hands on him. "Brother Saul," he said, "the Lord has sent me – Jesus himself, who appeared to you on the road as you were coming here. He sent me so that you might see again and be filled with the Holy Spirit." At once something like fish scales fell from Saul's eyes, and he was able to see again. He stood up and was baptised; and after he had eaten, his strength came back.

1. READING

What is going on?

Read the text and ask, what is going on? What strikes you about this passage? Details? Actions?

Possible prompts:

- Saul on a mission striking terror.
- A divine light in Damascus startles him.
- Who are you, Lord?
- "I am Jesus whom you persecute."
- What would Ananias have been thinking?
- "Brother Saul," Ananias said.
- Paul sees God's way; is converted; is baptised.

2. REFLECTION

What does it mean for us?

Read the text again. What phrase do you like in the text and why? What word attracts you? How does the text speak to you in the various places and situations you find yourself?

Possible prompts:

- Have we ever set out deliberately to do something wrong?
- Has God ever changed our minds for us, by some sudden light or inspiration?
- People, like Ananias, can change our hearts.
- Repentance is a good feeling.

3. RESPONSE

Making some prayers

Read the text again. We have heard God's Word and we have tried to see what it means. We can talk to Jesus about his message. It can be a prayer you know or one you make up.

Possible prompts:

- If we need it, startle us into greater love and service.
- Make us open to receive help from others that you send to us.
- Change the hearts of all planning to do evil.
- Give us grace to see what needs changing in our lives and our world.
- When we see persons or things wrongly, heal our blindness.
- Lord, Jesus Christ, have mercy on me, a sinner.

4. REST

Enjoy the text

Read the text again.

Pause – a minute or two of silence with the text.

Invite pupils to take away a few words from this time of reflection, prayer or meditation as a message for today.

- "Saul, Saul, why are you persecuting me."
- "Who are you, Lord?"

A CONCLUDING PRAYER

May he support us all day long
Till the shadows lengthen and evening comes,
And the busy world is hushed,
And the fever of life is over,
And our work is done.
Then, in his mercy,
may he give us safe lodging,
And a holy rest and peace at last.

John Henry Newman

The good life

INTRODUCTION

■ *Scripture*: The prophet Micah preached in the decades before 700 BC. It was a time of great moral corruption and injustice everywhere in society, so that the poor and the weak were utterly oppressed. Through the prophet God threatens his people and calls on them to change their ways. What he requires is not more empty religious practices, but a profound change of heart and of behaviour.

■ *Here I Am*: People rejoice in freedom; many nations struggle for it. It is a great blessing, but it also carries responsibility. We are called upon to use our freedom wisely and having regard to others. The text, one of the best-known and best-loved of the Old Testament, shows us how to live in responsible freedom.

SCRIPTURE   Micah 6: 6-8

WHAT SHALL I BRING to the Lord, the God of heaven, when I come to worship him? Shall I bring the best calves to burn as offerings to him? Will the Lord be pleased if I bring him thousands of sheep or endless streams of olive-oil? Shall I offer him my first-born child to pay for my sins? No, the Lord has told us what is good. What he requires of us is this: to do what is just, to show constant love, and to live in humble fellowship with our God.

1. READING

What is going on?

Read the text and ask, what is going on? What strikes you about this passage? Details? Actions?

Possible prompts:

- How can sinners come to God?
- What could people offer an angry God?
- God rejects elaborate sacrifices.
- What does God consider good and want from us?

2. REFLECTION

What does it mean for us?

Read the text again. What phrase do you like in the text and why? What word attracts you? How does the text speak to you in the various places and situations you find yourself?

Possible prompts:

- What is in our heart when we come to pray?
- Is God interested at all in what we could offer?
- How do we "do what is just"?
- How do we "show constant love"?
- How do we "live in humble fellowship with our God"?
- God wants our responsible freedom.

3. RESPONSE

Making some prayers

Read the text again. We have heard God's Word and we have tried to see what it means. We can talk to Jesus about his message. It can be a prayer you know or one you make up.

Possible prompts:

- Free us from all that holds us back from loving you.
- Show us your way, O Lord.
- Help us to do what is just.
- Teach us to show constant love.
- Show us how to walk in humble fellowship.
- Lord, by your Cross and Resurrection you have set us free.

4. REST

Enjoy the text

Read the text again.

Pause – a minute or two of silence with the text.

Invite pupils to take away a few words from this time of reflection, prayer or meditation as a message for today.

- "To act justly, to love tenderly, to walk humbly with your God."

(RSV trans.)

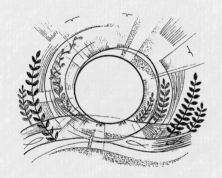

A CONCLUDING PRAYER

Most merciful Redeemer,
friend and brother;
May I know you more clearly,
Love you more dearly,
and follow you more nearly,
Day by day.

St Richard of Chichester

Sin and repentance

INTRODUCTION

■ *Scripture*: Sometime after 1000 BC David was king and richly blessed by God. Despite all he had, he coveted the wife of his great warrior Uriah. He had him killed so that he could marry her. Through the prophet God reveals to David the nature of his terrible crimes. The king repents.

■ *Here I Am*: There are few of us who have not broken friendships, upset others, been hurtful or unreasonable. We can easily pass it off and not recognise that we are in the wrong. We may not at all appreciate being told of our faults. But we need others to build bridges, to heal relationships, to show us the way back to God, to repent and be healed. The difficulty arises not when we fail ourselves but when others show us their failures and hurt us in doing so.

SCRIPTURE   2 Samuel 12: 1-9, 12-13

THE LORD sent the prophet Nathan to David. Nathan went to him and said, "There were two men who lived in the same town; one was rich and the other poor. The rich man had many cattle and sheep, while the poor man had only one lamb, which he had bought. He took care of it, and it grew up in his home with his children. He would feed it with some of his own food, let it drink from his cup, and hold it in his lap. The lamb was like a daughter to him. One day a visitor arrived at the rich man's home. The rich man didn't want to kill one of his own animals to prepare a meal for him; instead, he took the poor man's lamb and cooked a meal for his guest." David was very angry with the rich man and said, "I swear by the living Lord that the man who did this ought to die! For having done such a cruel thing, he must pay back four times as much as he took" "You are that man," Nathan said to David. "And this is what the Lord God of Israel says: 'I made you king of Israel and rescued you from Saul. I gave you his kingdom and his wives; I made you king over Israel and Judah. If this had not been enough, I would have given you twice as much. Why, then, have you disobeyed my commands? You had Uriah killed in battle; you let the Ammonites kill him and then you took his wife!'... You sinned in secret, but I will make this [trouble] happen in broad daylight for all Israel to see.' " "I have sinned against the Lord," David said. Nathan replied, "The Lord forgives you, you will not die."

1. READING

What is going on?

Read the text and ask, what is going on? What strikes you about this passage? Details? Actions?

Possible prompts:

- Nathan's parable of the lamb.
- David could not see his great sin.
- The Lord was generous to David.
- David wanted still more and his thoughts led him to murder an innocent soldier.
- Nathan leads David to the Lord's mercy.

2. REFLECTION

What does it mean for us?

Read the text again. What phrase do you like in the text and why? What word attracts you? How does the text speak to you in the various places and situations you find yourself?

Possible prompts:

- Sometimes we cannot see the evil we do.
- Others can help us to appreciate our wrongdoing and see a way out of it.
- The Lord is generous with mercy for us.
- The danger of dwelling on negative or evil desires.
- We can be bridge-builders and help others to come into freedom and peace.

3. RESPONSE

Making some prayers

Read the text again. We have heard God's Word and we have tried to see what it means. We can talk to Jesus about his message. It can be a prayer you know or one you make up.

Possible prompts:

- Help us to forgive others and ourselves.
- Show us how to help others in a sensitive way.
- Help us to build bridges for others, with others, to others.
- Help us to be more satisfied with what we have.

4. REST

Enjoy the text

Read the text again.
Pause – a minute or two of silence with the text. Invite pupils to take away a few words from this time of reflection, prayer or meditation as a message for today.

- To see ourselves with truth.
- The beauty and wonder of forgiveness and mercy.

A CONCLUDING PRAYER

Lord, make me a channel of your peace;
where there is hatred let me sow love,
where there is injury let me sow pardon,
where there is doubt let me sow faith,
where there is despair let me give hope,
where there is darkness let me give light,
where there is sadness let me give joy.
O Divine Master, grant that I may
not try to be comforted but to comfort,
not try to be understood but to understand,
not try to be loved but to love.
For it is in giving that we receive,
it is in forgiving that we are forgiven,
and it is in dying that we are born to eternal life.

Prayer attributed to St Francis

Peter's sermon

INTRODUCTION

■ *Scripture*: On Pentecost day Peter spoke to the people of Jerusalem. His sermon was a summary of God's plan of death, resurrection and sending the Spirit. The people are horrified to be told they have killed God's Holy One, the Messiah. But Peter reassures them that all they need do is repent and believe.

■ *Here I Am*: There is an urgency about telling and spreading good news. It has been said that good news travels fast. In this text we have the core of the Gospel: almost everything in Christianity can be reduced to this text.

SCRIPTURE

Acts 2: 14, 32-33, 36-42

THEN PETER STOOD UP with the other eleven apostles and in a loud voice began to speak to the crowd: "Fellow-Jews and all of you who live in Jerusalem, listen to me and let me tell you what this means. God has raised this very Jesus from death, and we are all witnesses to this fact. He has been raised to the right-hand side of God, his Father, and has received from him the Holy Spirit, as he had promised. What you now see and hear is his gift that he has poured out on us. All the people of Israel, then, are to know for sure that this Jesus, whom you crucified, is the one that God has made Lord and Messiah!" When the people heard this, they were deeply troubled and said to Peter and the other apostles, "What shall we do, brothers?" Peter said to them, "Each one of you must turn away from his sins and be baptised in the name of Jesus Christ, so that your sins will be forgiven; and you will receive God's gift, the Holy Spirit. For God's promise was made to you and your children, and to all who are far away – all whom the Lord our God calls to himself." Peter made his appeal to them and with many other words he urged them, saying, "Save yourselves from the punishment coming on this wicked people!" Many of them believed his message and were baptised, and about three thousand people were added to the group that day. They spent their time in learning from the apostles, taking part in the fellowship, and sharing in the fellowship meals and the prayers.

1. READING

What is going on?

Read the text and ask, what is going on? What strikes you about this passage? Details? Actions?

Possible prompts:

- Peter explaining God's plan.
- That God raised Jesus from the dead.
- He sent the Holy Spirit.
- The great sin of killing the Messiah: what to do now?
- Turn away from sin and receive the Holy Spirit.
- The new life of believers: learning about God's plan, sharing in fellowship, the Lord's Supper and the prayers.

2. REFLECTION

What does it mean for us?

Read the text again. What phrase do you like in the text and why? What word attracts you? How does the text speak to you in the various places and situations you find yourself?

Possible prompts:

- The centre of our faith: Calvary, Easter, and Pentecost.
- Good news for us, and for others.
- How can we share it with others?
- Constant turning from sin and continual receiving the Holy Spirit.
- Would people think our lives and word are convincing?

3. RESPONSE

Making some prayers

Read the text again. We have heard God's Word and we have tried to see what it means. We can talk to Jesus about his message. It can be a prayer you know or one you make up.

Possible prompts:

- Thank you, Father, for your plan of salvation.
- May we love the mysteries of salvation in the Apostles' Creed.
- Give us all the courage of St Peter and others.
- May we be eager to learn about the faith.
- Make us generous in fellowship, in sharing our life and faith with others. Make us constant in prayer.

4. REST

Enjoy the text

Read the text again.

Pause – a minute or two of silence with the text.

Invite pupils to take away a few words from this time of reflection, prayer or meditation as a message for today.

- Let us proclaim the Mystery of Faith.
- Teaching, fellowship, Eucharist, prayer.

A CONCLUDING PRAYER

I shall pass through this world but once.
Any good thing that I can do,
or any kindness that I can show
to any person whatsoever,
let me do it now, and not defer it,
For I shall not pass this way again.

Sent on mission

INTRODUCTION

■ *Scripture*: Jesus ascends to glory after forty days. He leaves the Church with a mission to spread his teaching. But they are to await the power of the Holy Spirit who will complete Jesus' work and prepare them for their mission to the whole world.

■ *Here I Am*: Messengers are important but they are even more powerful when they witness personally to what they say. To be effective messengers or credible witnesses, we need the power of the Holy Spirit.

SCRIPTURE

Acts 1: 3-8

FOR FORTY DAYS after his death he appeared to them many times in ways that proved beyond doubt that he was alive. They saw him, and he talked with them about the Kingdom of God. And when they came together, he gave them this order: "Do not leave Jerusalem, but wait for the gift I told you about, the gift my Father promised. John baptised with water but in a few days you will be baptised with the Holy Spirit".

When the apostles met together with Jesus, they asked him, "Lord, will you at this time give the Kingdom back to Israel?" Jesus said to them, "The times and occasions are set by my Father's own authority, and it is not for you to know when they will be. But when the Holy Spirit comes upon you, you will be filled with power, and you will be witnesses for me in Jerusalem, in all Judaea and Samaria, and to the ends of the earth."

1. READING

What is going on?

Read the text and ask, what is going on? What strikes you about this passage? Details? Actions?

Possible prompts:

- The farewell meeting between Jesus and his apostles after his Resurrection.
- He is departing.
- He wants them to be ready for a mission to the world.
- They are to await the Holy Spirit in Jerusalem.
- "You will be my witnesses..."

2. REFLECTION

What does it mean for us?

Read the text again. What phrase do you like in the text and why? What word attracts you? How does the text speak to you in the various places and situations you find yourself?

Possible prompts:

- Jesus meets us in various ways.
- He instructs us.
- Jesus promises the Holy Spirit to his workers.
- Jesus constantly wants to baptise us, to plunge us into his Holy Spirit.
- What sort of messengers and witness are we?

3. RESPONSE

Making some prayers

Read the text again. We have heard God's Word and we have tried to see what it means. We can talk to Jesus about his message. It can be a prayer you know or one you make up.

Possible prompts:

- Jesus is Lord.
- I believe in the Holy Spirit.
- Send us your Spirit.
- Make us bold and fearless in proclaiming your message.
- Thank you for the gift of your good news.
- Support all who spread your message faithfully.

4. REST

Enjoy the text

Read the text again.
Pause – a minute or two of silence with the text.
Invite pupils to take away a few words from this time of reflection, prayer or meditation as a message for today.

- The message from Jerusalem to the ends of the earth.
- The power of the Holy Spirit.

A CONCLUDING PRAYER

Come, Holy Spirit,
fill the hearts of all of us.
Enkindle in us
the fire of your love.
Send forth your Spirit
and you will be created
and renew the face of the earth.

Pentecost

INTRODUCTION

■ *Scripture*: The climax of God's plan was the coming of the Holy Spirit to complete and spread the work of Jesus. On the Jewish feast of Pentecost the Holy Spirit came on the Church, making the disciples of Jesus strong and transforming their way of life in the Christian community.

■ *Here I Am*: We all know the difficulty of a power-failure. All the things we take for granted are now impossible. On a personal level most of us have experienced moments when we lack energy. It may be that we have been working too hard, have been unwell or just generally out of sorts. With rest and good food our energy levels can be restored. In our spiritual journey we need the energy that comes from God's Spirit.

SCRIPTURE

Acts 2: 1-4, 42-47

WHEN THE DAY of Pentecost came, all the believers were gathered together in one place. Suddenly there was a noise from the sky which sounded like a strong wind blowing, and it filled the whole house where they were sitting. Then they saw what looked like tongues of fire which spread out and touched each person there. They were all filled with the Holy Spirit and began to talk in other languages, as the Spirit enabled them to speak... They spent their time in learning from the apostles, taking part in the fellowship, and sharing in the fellowship meals and the prayers. Many miracles and wonders were being done through the apostles, and everyone was filled with awe. All the believers continued together in close fellowship and shared their belongings with one another, they would sell their property and possessions, and distribute the money among all, according to what each one needed. Day after day they met as a group in the Temple, and they had their meals together in their homes, eating with glad and humble hearts, praising God and enjoying the good will of all the people. And every day the Lord added to their group those who were being saved.

1. READING

What is going on?

Read the text and ask, what is going on? What strikes you about this passage? Details? Actions?

Possible prompts:

- The apostles and believers suddenly receive the Holy Spirit.
- This sudden outpouring of God's Spirit gives them new power and energy.
- They began to talk in different languages.
- Many miracles and wonders.
- The believers were moved by a new generosity, sharing their belongings.
- The life of the community: teaching, sharing, Eucharist, prayer, miracles, generosity.
- God added daily to their group.

2. REFLECTION

What does it mean for us?

Read the text again. What phrase do you like in the text and why? What word attracts you? How does the text speak to you in the various places and situations you find yourself?

Possible prompts:

- Our need for God's power and energy.
- Treasuring the sacraments of baptism, confirmation and Eucharist.
- What are the signs in our lives of the divine energy we have received?
- What we can learn from the apostles?
- The generous life-style of the believer.
- Are we good sharers?

3. RESPONSE

Making some prayers

Read the text again. We have heard God's Word and we have tried to see what it means. We can talk to Jesus about his message. It can be a prayer you know or one you make up.

Possible prompts:

- Thank you for faith, hope and love, for the gift of community.
- Thank you Lord for the sacraments which give us and our Church the divine energy of the Holy Spirit.
  - * Baptism and Confirmation
  - * Reconciliation.
  - * Eucharist.
  - * The Sacrament of the Sick.
  - * Marriage and Holy Orders.
- Thank you for the fruits of the Holy Spirit:
  - * Love, joy peace.
  - * Patience, kindness, goodness.
  - * Faithfulness, humility and self-control.

4. REST

Enjoy the text

Read the text again.
Pause – a minute or two of silence with the text.
Invite pupils to take away a few words from this time of reflection, prayer or meditation as a message for today.

- All filled with the Holy Spirit.
- Learning from the apostles, sharing in meals, in the Eucharist and the prayers.
- Day by day they met, praising God and enjoying the good will of people.

A CONCLUDING PRAYER

"Send your Holy Spirit upon them
To be their Helper and Guide.
Give them the spirit of wisdom and understanding,
the Spirit of right judgement and courage,
The Spirit of wonder and awe in your presence".

Liturgy of Confirmation

The Lord's Day

Here I Am: HOLIDAYS – HOLY DAYS

INTRODUCTION

■ *Scripture*: God, we read, rested on the seventh day of creation, and so made this day holy. It was a day for physical rest, for worship and for spiritual reflection. By the time of Jesus the Pharisees had made the Sabbath not a joyful day but one that was burdensome, loaded with restrictions. Jesus returns people to the true meaning of the Sabbath.

■ *Here I Am*: Holidays (originally "holy days") are opportunities to recover, to be still, to be re-energised and to pause from the frenzy of life and business that can overtake us. It is also important to have a special day for worship.

SCRIPTURE

Mark 3: 23-27

JESUS WAS WALKING through some cornfields on the Sabbath. As his disciples walked along with him, they began to pick the ears of corn. So the Pharisees said to Jesus, "Look, it is against our Law for your disciples to do that on the Sabbath!" Jesus answered, "Have you never read what David did that time when he needed something to eat? He and his men were hungry, so he went into the house of God and ate the bread offered to God. This happened when Abiathar was the High Priest. According to our Law only the priests may eat this bread – but David ate it and even gave it to his men." And Jesus concluded, "The Sabbath was made for the good of man; man was not made for the Sabbath. So the Son of Man is Lord even of the Sabbath."

1. READING

What is going on?

Read the text and ask, what is going on? What strikes you about this passage? Details? Actions?

Possible prompts:

- Jesus is walking through some cornfields on the Sabbath.
- His disciples innocently picking ears of corn.
- The Pharisees take offence.

- They were trying to catch Jesus out.
- Jesus springs to his disciples' defence.
- Goodness and the well-being of persons comes before the law.
- The Son of Man is Lord of the Sabbath.

2. REFLECTION

What does it mean for us?

Read the text again. What phrase do you like in the text and why? What word attracts you? How does the text speak to you in the various places and situations you find yourself?

Possible prompts:

- What is most important for us on the Sabbath?
- Is our Sunday like every other day?
- Sunday to be again somehow the Lord's Day.
- Criticising other people is not very fruitful.

3. RESPONSE

Making some prayers

Read the text again. We have heard God's Word and we have tried to see what it means. We can talk to Jesus about his message. It can be a prayer you know or one you make up.

Possible prompts:

- Thank you, Lord, for Sundays and rest days.
- Thank you for holidays and leisure times.
- Help us to keep Sundays holy and peaceful.
- Bless all who are too busy to give you time.
- Help priests, catechists and families to bring us closer to you.

4. REST

Enjoy the text

Read the text again.

Pause – a minute or two of silence with the text. Invite pupils to take away a few words from this time of reflection, prayer or meditation as a message for today.

- Sabbath rest.
- Jesus putting people first.

A CONCLUDING PRAYER

Glory to God in the highest,
And peace to his people on earth.
Lord God, Heavenly King,
Almighty God and Father,
We worship you,
We give you thanks,
We praise you for your glory.

Also by Jude Groden RSM and Christopher O'Donnell O.CARM

 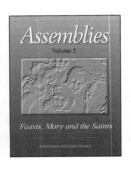 

Assemblies – Volume 1
Liturgical seasons and school occasions

Size: A4 (11 3/4" x 8") / 104 pages / Two colour throughout / Illustrated / ISBN 0 85597 615 2

Assemblies – Volume 2
Feasts, Mary and the Saints

Size: A4 (11 3/4" x 8") / 140 pages / Two colour throughout / Illustrated / ISBN 0 85597 617 9

St Patrick, Spirit and Prayer
Jude Groden RSM

This little book includes the prayers of one of the most remarkable saints of early Christendom. Plus a Prayer Service for schools and an essay on Patrick's spirituality by Christopher O'Donnell.

Size: 115 x 180mm / 32 pages / Colour photographs / ISBN 0 85597 637 3

Available from: **McCrimmon Publishing Co. Ltd.**